OECD Tax Policy Studies

The Role and Design of Net Wealth Taxes in the OECD

No.26

Please cite this publication as:
OECD (2018), *The Role and Design of Net Wealth Taxes in the OECD*, OECD Tax Policy Studies, No.26, OECD Publishing, Paris.
http://dx.doi.org/10.1787/9789264290303-en

ISBN 978-92-64-29029-7 (print)
ISBN 978-92-64-29030-3 (PDF)

Series: OECD Tax Policy Studies
ISSN 1990-0546 (print)
ISSN 1990-0538 (online)

Photo credits: Cover © selensergen/Thinkstock.

Corrigenda to OECD publications may be found on line at: *www.oecd.org/about/publishing/corrigenda.htm*.

Foreword

This report examines and assesses the current and historical use of net wealth taxes, defined as recurrent taxes on individual net assets, in OECD countries. It provides background on the use of wealth taxes over time in OECD countries as well as on trends in income and wealth inequality. It then assesses the case for and against the use of a net wealth tax to raise revenues and reduce inequality, based on efficiency, equity and tax administration considerations. The effects of personal capital income taxes and taxes on wealth transfers are also discussed to understand how these taxes interact with net wealth taxes. Finally, the report looks at practical tax design issues and shows that the way a net wealth tax is designed can have a significant impact on the effectiveness and fairness of the tax. The report concludes with a number of practical tax policy recommendations regarding net wealth taxes.

This report complements recent OECD work on the taxation of household savings and, more broadly, on tax design for inclusive growth. The report also paves the way for future work focusing, among other areas, on the design of inheritance and capital gains taxes, as well as on the potential use of wealth-testing for broader tax and benefit purposes.

Acknowledgments

This report was produced by the Tax Policy and Statistics Division of the OECD Centre for Tax Policy and Administration with the financial support of the Korea Institute of Public Finance (KIPF).

The report was written by Sarah Perret. Guidance and critical input were provided by Bert Brys. The report has also benefited from contributions by Pierce O'Reilly and Alastair Thomas and helpful comments by David Bradbury, Head of the Tax Policy and Statistics Division at the OECD. The author would also like to thank the delegates of the Working Party No.2 on Tax Policy Analysis and Tax Statistics for their responses to the "OECD Questionnaire on Current and Historical Net Wealth Taxes" and for their feedback on the report. Raphaëlle Gerno's assistance with background research and Bethany Millar-Powell's help with graphs and tables are also gratefully acknowledged. Carrie Tyler assisted with the publication process. Violet Sochay provided administrative assistance.

Table of contents

Tables

Figures

Boxes

Executive summary

Net wealth taxes are far less widespread than they used to be in the OECD but there has recently been a renewed interest in wealth taxation. While 12 countries had net wealth taxes in 1990, there were only four OECD countries that still levied recurrent taxes on individuals' net wealth in 2017. Decisions to repeal net wealth taxes have often been justified by efficiency and administrative concerns and by the observation that net wealth taxes have frequently failed to meet their redistributive goals. The revenues collected from net wealth taxes have also, with a few exceptions, been very low. More recently, however, some countries have shown a renewed interest in net wealth taxes as a way to raise revenues and address wealth inequality.

This report seeks to answer four main questions:

- Is there a rationale for addressing wealth inequality through the tax system?
- If so, is a net wealth tax the most appropriate instrument to address wealth inequality?
- What have been the practical experiences of countries that currently have or previously had a net wealth tax?
- Where a country has decided to implement a net wealth tax, how should it be designed to maximise efficiency and equity and minimise tax administration and compliance costs?

The report argues that there is a strong case for addressing wealth inequality through the tax system. Wealth inequality is far greater than income inequality, and there is some evidence suggesting that wealth inequality has increased in recent decades. In addition, wealth accumulation operates in a self-reinforcing way and is likely to increase in the absence of taxation. High earners are able to save more, meaning that they are able to invest more and ultimately accumulate more wealth. Moreover, investment returns tend to increase with wealth, largely because wealthy taxpayers are in a better position to invest in riskier assets and generally have higher levels of financial education, expertise and access to professional investment advice.

While the tax system should help address wealth inequality, the question is whether a wealth tax is the most effective way to do so. The report assesses the case for and against net wealth taxes, looking at efficiency, equity and administrative arguments. It also compares the effects of net wealth taxes with personal capital income taxes and taxes on wealth transfers.

Overall, the report concludes that from both an efficiency and equity perspective, there are limited arguments for having a net wealth tax in addition to broad-based personal capital income taxes and well-designed inheritance and gift taxes. While there are important similarities between personal capital income taxes and net wealth taxes, the report shows that net wealth taxes tend to be more distortive and less equitable. This is largely because they are imposed irrespective of the actual returns that taxpayers earn on their assets. The report also argues that capital income taxes alone will most likely not be enough to address wealth inequality and suggests the need to complement capital income taxes with a form of wealth taxation. The report finds that there is a strong case for an accompanying inheritance tax on efficiency, equity and administrative grounds.

However, the report finds that there are stronger arguments for having a net wealth tax in the absence of broad-based personal capital income taxes and taxes on wealth transfers. Where the overall tax burden on capital is low, or where levying broad-based capital income taxes or inheritance taxes is not feasible, net wealth taxes may play an important substitution role. The report shows how a net wealth tax can serve as an imperfect substitute for taxes on personal capital income, on capital gains or on wealth transfers.

More generally, the report suggests that the merits of a net wealth tax cannot be assessed in isolation but depend on a country's overall tax system and broader economic and social circumstances. Previous OECD work has already highlighted the need to look at tax systems as a whole and in the context of countries' economic and social circumstances. For instance, a net wealth tax may have more limited distortive effects and be more justified as a way to enhance progressivity in countries where the taxation of personal capital income is comparatively low. In practice, this implies that in countries with dual income tax systems that tax capital income at flat (and often low) rates or in countries where capital gains are not taxed, there may be a stronger justification for levying a net wealth tax. A similar argument can be made for countries that do not levy taxes on inheritances. Beyond tax considerations, there might also be greater justification for a net wealth tax in a country exhibiting high levels of wealth inequality as a way to narrow wealth gaps at a faster pace.

Finally, the report provides a number of concrete tax design recommendations for countries that already implement or have decided to introduce a net wealth tax. Where a net wealth tax exists in addition to broad-based capital income taxes, tax exemption thresholds should be high to ensure that the net wealth tax is only levied on the very wealthy. Tax rates should be low and take into account tax rates on capital income to avoid imposing excessively high tax burdens on capital so as to prevent capital flight. In the absence of broad-based capital income taxes, lower exemption thresholds and higher tax rates may be justified in the design of the net wealth tax. Tax rates should be progressive, especially in cases where net wealth taxes are not in addition to broad-based capital income taxes and/or wealth transfer taxes, to enhance the overall tax system's progressivity.

Other net wealth tax design recommendations include:

- Limiting tax exemptions and reliefs;
- Exempting business assets, with clear criteria restricting eligibility;
- Exempting personal and household effects up to a certain value;
- Aligning the tax base with asset market values;
- Keeping the value of hard-to-value assets or the value of taxpayers' total net wealth constant for a few years to avoid yearly reassessments;
- Allowing debts to be deductible only if they have been incurred to acquire taxable assets – or, if the tax exemption threshold is high, consider further limiting debt deductibility;
- Allowing payments in instalments for taxpayers facing liquidity constraints;
- Ensuring transparency in the treatment of assets held in trusts;
- Continuing efforts to enhance tax transparency and exchange information on the assets that residents hold in other jurisdictions;

- Developing third-party reporting;
- Establishing rules to prevent international double wealth taxation; and
- Regularly evaluating the effects of the wealth tax.

Chapter 1. Overview of individual net wealth taxes in OECD countries

This chapter provides an overview of individual net wealth taxes in OECD countries. It looks at how the number of countries levying a net wealth tax has evolved over time. It also examines trends in the revenues that have been collected from net wealth taxes since the mid-1960s.

The statistical data for Israel are supplied by and under the responsibility of the relevant Israeli authorities. The use of such data by the OECD is without prejudice to the status of the Golan Heights, East Jerusalem and Israeli settlements in the West Bank under the terms of international law.

This chapter is based on the tax rules that were in place as of 1 September 2017. Since then, France has replaced its net wealth tax ("*impôt de solidarité sur la fortune*") with a new real estate wealth tax ("*impôt sur la fortune immobilière*"), with effect from 1 January 2018.

This chapter provides an overview of net wealth taxes paid by individuals in OECD countries. It examines the declining prevalence of net wealth taxes in OECD countries and looks at how wealth tax revenues have evolved over time. Generally, this chapter shows that net wealth taxes are far less popular than they used to be – with only four OECD countries levying such taxes in 2017. Concerns about their efficiency and administrative costs, in particular in comparison to the limited revenues they tend to generate, have led to their repeal in many countries. More recently, however, trends in income and wealth inequality, combined with the need to balance public budgets, have led to a renewed interest in wealth taxes.

Very few OECD countries still have net wealth taxes

Net wealth taxes are recurrent taxes on individual net wealth stocks. They include national and subnational recurrent taxes on a wide range of movable and immovable property, net of debt. They are distinct from other taxes on capital, including taxes on capital income and taxes on wealth transfers. They can also be distinguished from other taxes on wealth stocks: compared to recurrent taxes on immovable property, they are taxes on a broad range of property and debts are deductible; and unlike sporadic capital levies, net wealth taxes are levied on a regular basis (usually annually).

The number of OECD countries levying individual net wealth taxes dropped from 12 in 1990 to 4 in 2017 (Figure 1.1). There are many OECD countries that used to have wealth taxes but that repealed them in the 1990s and 2000s including Austria (in 1994), Denmark (in 1997), Germany (in 1997), the Netherlands (in 2001), Finland, Iceland, Luxembourg (all three in 2006) and Sweden (in 2007). In 2008, although it did not technically repeal its wealth tax, Spain introduced a 100% tax credit, reducing all taxpayers' wealth tax liabilities to zero. After the crisis, however, both Iceland and Spain reinstated net wealth taxes as temporary fiscal consolidation measures. In 2017, France, Norway, Spain and Switzerland were the only OECD countries that levied net wealth taxes.

Figure 1.1. Evolution of the number of OECD countries levying individual net wealth taxes between 1990 and 2017

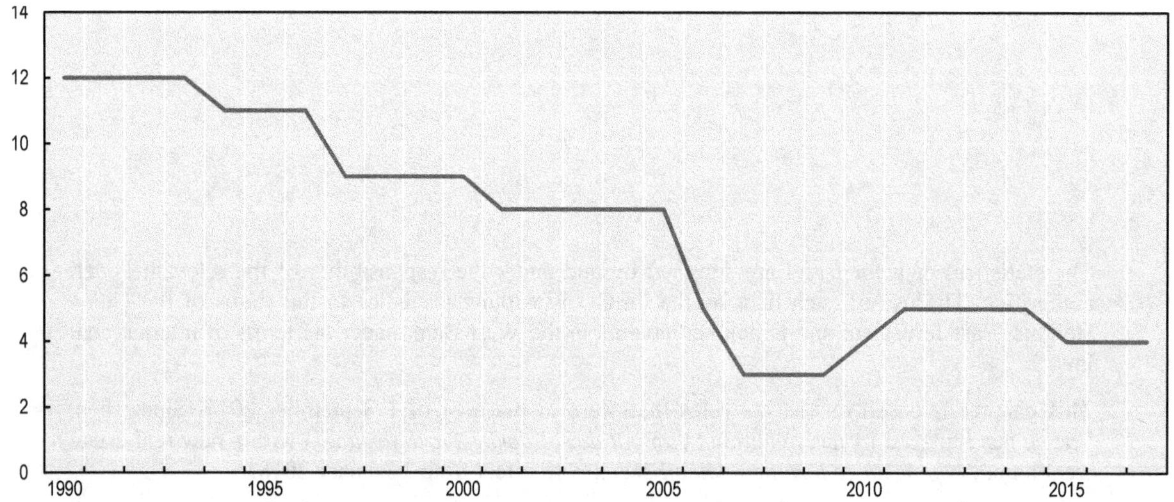

Source: OECD Net Wealth Tax Questionnaire

Many factors have been put forward to justify the repeal of net wealth taxes. The main arguments relate to their efficiency costs and the risks of capital flight, in particular in light of increased capital mobility and wealthy taxpayers' access to tax havens; the observation that net wealth taxes often failed to meet their redistributive goals as a result of their narrow tax bases as well as tax avoidance and evasion; and concerns about their high administrative and compliance costs, in particular compared to their limited revenues (i.e. high cost-yield ratio). To some extent, the limited revenues collected from wealth taxes have made their elimination more acceptable and feasible from a political point of view (Kopczuk, 2012).

The repeal of net wealth taxes can also be viewed as part of a more general trend towards lowering tax rates on top income earners and capital. Indeed, there has been a steep decline in top personal income tax (PIT) rates over the past 30 years across the OECD. The OECD-wide average top statutory rate declined from 65.7% in 1981 to 50.6% in 1990 and to 41.4% in 2008 (Figure 1.2). The trend towards declining top PIT rates has nevertheless reversed slightly in recent years, with the average top PIT rate in the OECD reaching 43.3% in 2016. This reversal has been driven in large part by fiscal consolidation needs (OECD, 2016). At the same time, taxes on capital income have also fallen. Some countries introduced dual income tax systems which tax personal capital income at flat and lower rates compared to labour income. The unweighted average statutory CIT rate declined from 47% in 1981 to 24% in 2017; the unweighted average tax rate on dividend income for distributions of domestic source profits also fell from 75% to 42%. Finally, while inheritance and gift taxes are still applied rather widely (see below), several countries have reduced or abolished them since the mid-1990s. Overall, these changes have contributed to making OECD tax systems less progressive over the last three decades.

Figure 1.2. Combined top statutory personal income tax rates in OECD countries

Maximum, minimum and average, from 1981 to 2016

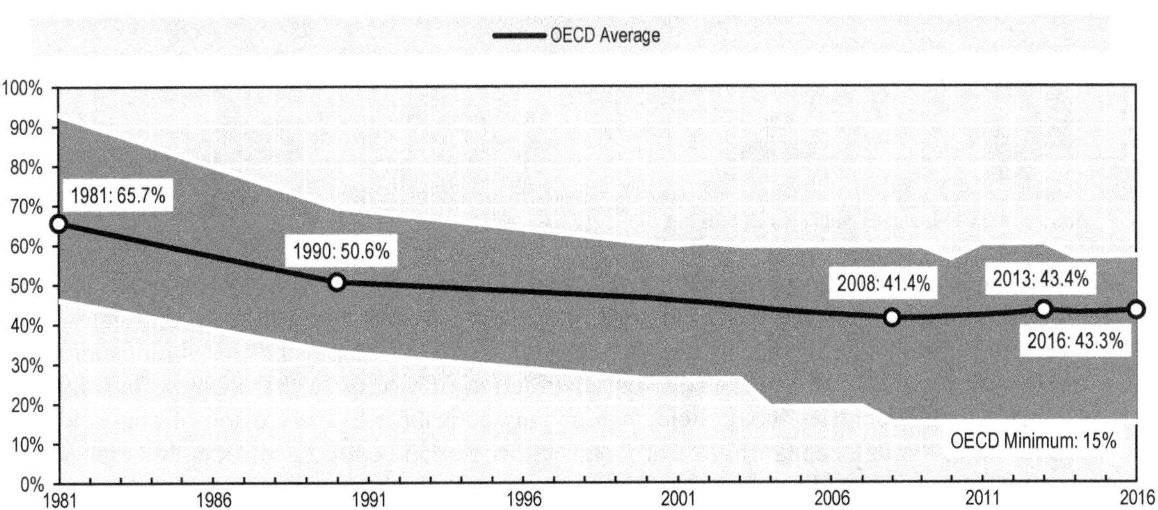

Note: Combined statutory rates include both central and sub-central tax rates
Source: OECD Tax Database

More recently, concerns about the highly unequal distribution of wealth, combined with the need for greater tax revenues in many countries, have led to a renewed interest in wealth taxes. Iceland, which had eliminated its net wealth tax in 2006, re-introduced it as a temporary "emergency" measure between 2010 and 2014. Spain, which had introduced a 100% wealth tax reduction in 2008, reinstated the net wealth tax in 2011. The reinstatement of the wealth tax was initially planned to be temporary but has been maintained since then. More generally from a practical perspective, tax administration improvements and the significant progress that has been achieved on international tax transparency and the exchange of information have made arguments against net wealth taxes on the grounds of their ineffectiveness less convincing (Iara, 2015).

Revenues from wealth taxes have typically been very low

Wealth taxes have generally accounted for a very small share of tax revenues. In 2016, tax revenues from individual net wealth taxes ranged from 0.2% of GDP in Spain to 1.0% of GDP in Switzerland. As a share of total tax revenues, they ranged from 0.5% in France to 3.7% in Switzerland (Figure 1.3). Looking at longer-term trends, Switzerland has always stood out as an exception, with tax revenues from individual net wealth taxes which have been consistently higher than in other countries (Figures 1.4 and 1.5).

Figure 1.3. Revenues from individual net wealth taxes in France, Norway, Spain and Switzerland in 2016

Revenues expressed as a share of GDP and as a share of total taxation

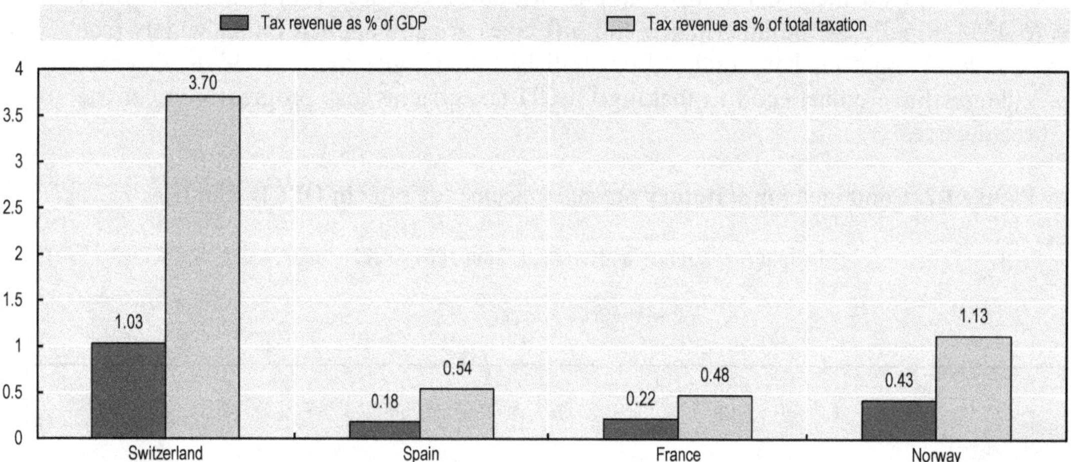

Source: OECD Revenue Statistics Database

Differences in individual net wealth tax revenues across countries reflect a variety of factors, including the design of the tax (e.g. taxed assets, tax schedule and rates, exemption thresholds, the tax treatment of debts) as well as taxpayers' possibilities and propensity to avoid and evade taxes, the distribution of wealth in the country, and the effects of other countries' tax policies, which may contribute to the erosion of domestic tax revenues through capital flight. For instance, Switzerland collects considerably higher revenues from its wealth taxes than other countries, which may be explained by tax design features such as comparatively low exemption thresholds and broader tax bases (see Chapter 4) as well as by the high share of wealthy individuals in the country. In Norway, on the other hand, despite relatively high tax rates and a low exemption threshold, revenues appear to be low. This may in part be because of the very favourable valuation rules that apply to primary residences for wealth tax purposes (see Chapter 4).

Over time, wealth tax revenues have generally not increased despite significant wealth growth

Looking at longer time periods, most of the countries that have or have had net wealth taxes experienced either stable or declining revenues from these taxes. Figure 1.4 compares net wealth tax revenues as a share of GDP in different years since 1980 in the countries that still had net wealth taxes in 2017. Figure 1.5 shows the evolution of revenues from all net wealth taxes, including both recurrent taxes on individual and corporate net wealth, since the mid-1960s in all the countries that used to have or still have net wealth taxes. Both figures show that tax revenue trends have differed across countries but that a majority of countries saw their revenues either remain stable or decline over time. Relatively stable long-term revenues from recurrent taxes on net wealth (although often volatile revenues in the short run) were observed in Austria, the Netherlands, Norway, Spain and Sweden while Denmark, Finland and Germany experienced declining net wealth tax revenues. On the other hand, France, Luxembourg and Switzerland have experienced tax revenue increases over time. In France and Switzerland, the increase in net wealth tax revenues was the result of an increase in revenues from individual net wealth taxes, while in Luxembourg the increase in revenues came from an increase in revenues from the corporate net wealth tax.

Figure 1.4. Revenues from individual net wealth taxes in France, Norway, Spain and Switzerland in different years

Revenues expressed as a share of GDP

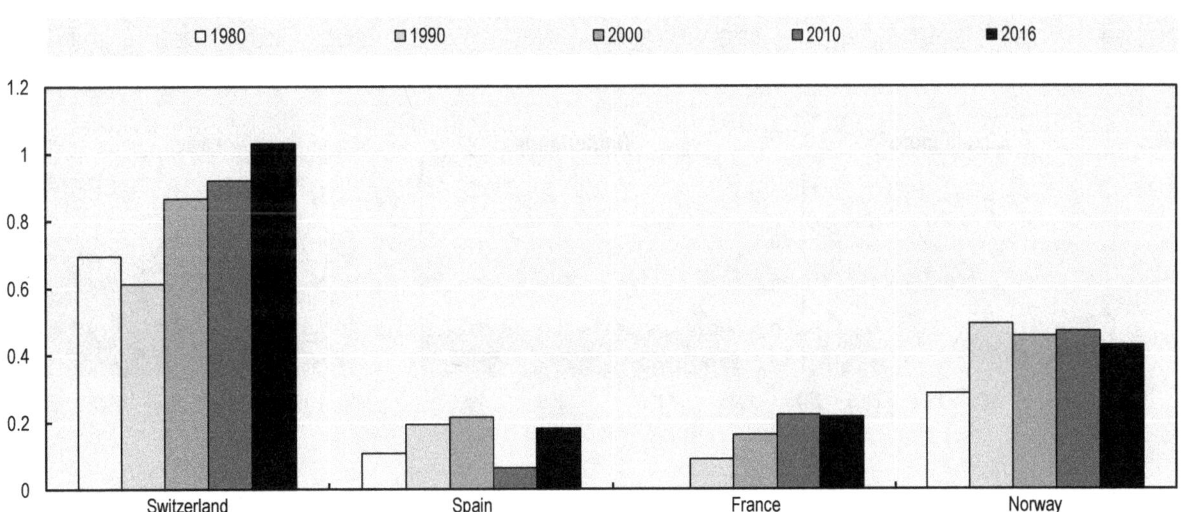

Source: OECD Revenue Statistics

Figure 1.5. Evolution of revenues from total net wealth taxes by country

Revenues expressed as a share of GDP

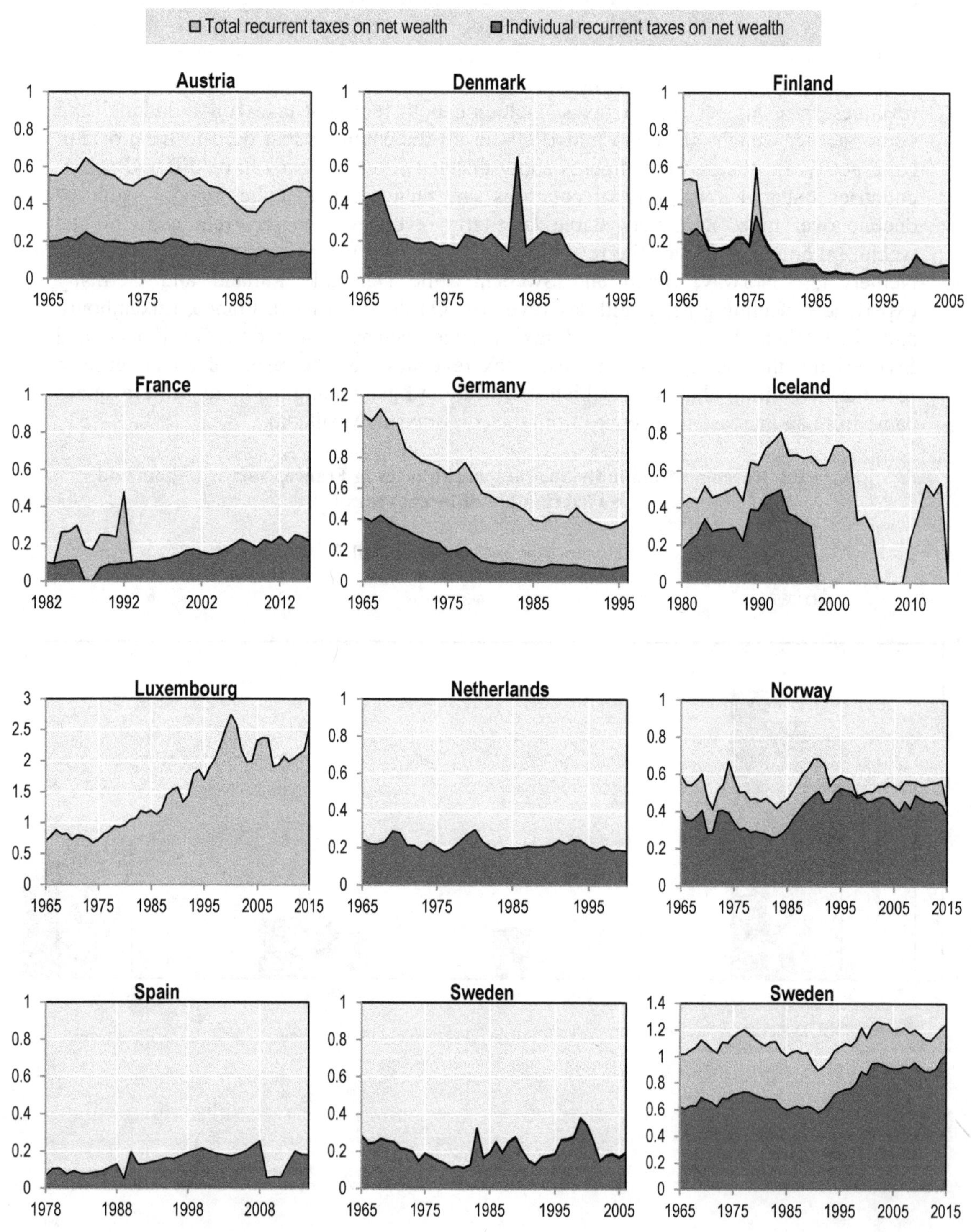

Source: OECD Revenue Statistics Database

Stable or declining net wealth tax revenues in most countries contrast with trends in wealth accumulation. There has been a rapid growth in wealth across countries. While trends are difficult to assess given the limited number of countries with reliable and comparable data, studies have shown that household net wealth has increased substantially over the last four decades in advanced countries. Figure 1.6 shows the significant increase in the average market-value national wealth per adult since 1970 in the United States, France, Germany and the United Kingdom. Using comparable data for 8 large advanced countries, Piketty and Zucman (2013) also find that the average ratio of net household wealth to national income increased by almost 80% between 1970 and 2010. This rapid growth in wealth has been explained, among other factors, by asset-price booms and a significant increase in private savings (IMF, 2014). However, wealth growth, which means that in theory the tax bases of net wealth taxes have expanded, has not translated into higher wealth tax revenues. This "paradox" is likely to be the result of changes in the design of net wealth taxes, the failure to update property values, as well as tax avoidance and evasion behaviours. Chapter 2 also suggests that there is evidence of increasing wealth inequality. This makes the fact that revenues from net wealth taxes, which are levied on the very wealthy, have not increased even more remarkable.

Figure 1.6. Average market-value national wealth per adult in France, Germany, the United Kingdom and the United States

Expressed in EUR ppp constant

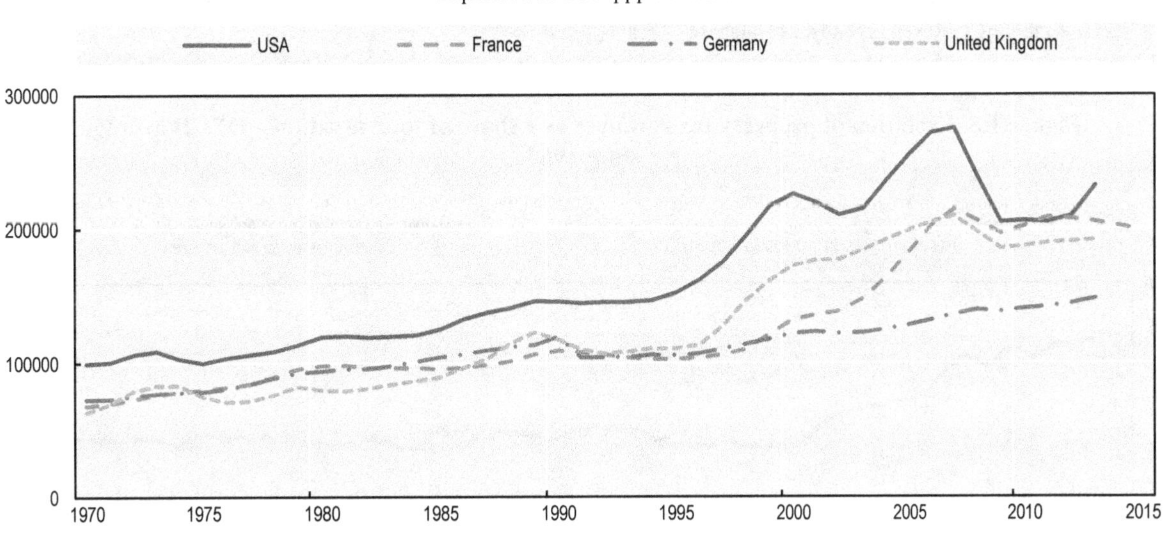

Source: World Wealth & Income Database

Other taxes on property play a bigger role than wealth taxes in OECD tax systems but overall property tax revenues remain limited

Wealth taxes tend to play a much less significant role than other types of taxes on property, in particular recurrent taxes on immovable property. Net wealth taxes are the least common form of property taxation across OECD countries. By contrast, Table 1 shows that recurrent taxes on immovable property, which are levied only on a portion of taxpayers' total capital stock as opposed to their total net wealth, are the most common form of property taxation and are in fact levied in all OECD countries. As shown in Figure 1.7, not only are recurrent taxes on immovable property very widely applied, but they are also generally by far the largest source of property tax revenues with a few exceptions – most notably Luxembourg and Switzerland.

Figure 1.7. Breakdown of property tax revenues in OECD countries in 2016

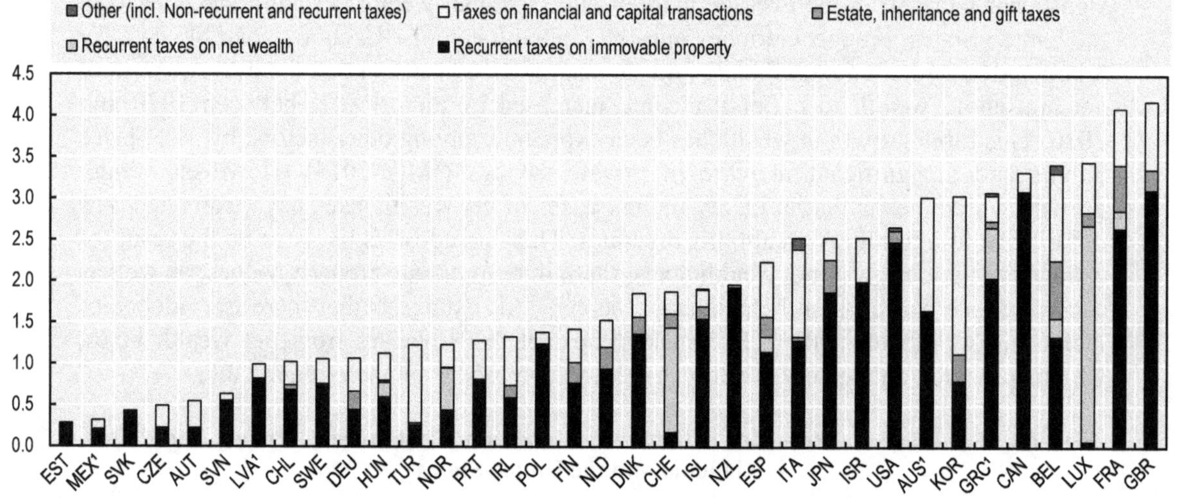

Note: 2015 data used for Australia, Greece, Latvia, and Mexico
Source: OECD Revenue Statistics Database

Figure 1.8. Evolution of property tax revenues as a share of total taxation – OECD average since 1965

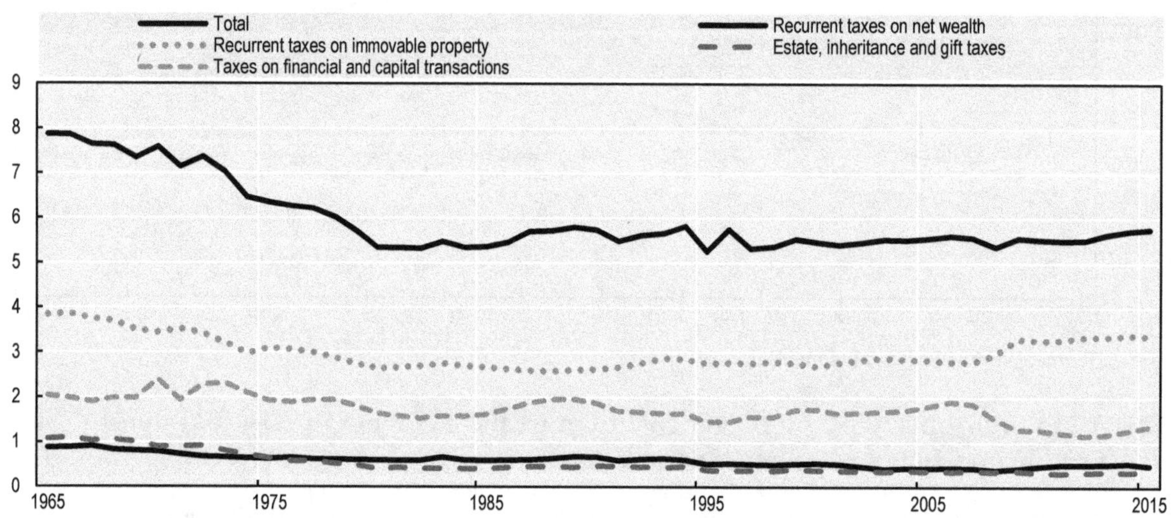

Source: OECD Revenue Statistics Database

Recurrent taxes on immovable property have a number of advantageous features. The tax base, and thus the revenue potential, is large as housing is the main form of wealth across households in all OECD countries (see Chapter 2). In addition, the immobility of the tax base limits potential behavioural responses to the tax and its visibility restricts avoidance and evasion opportunities. A recurrent immovable property tax can also act to some extent as a "benefits tax" and may have a smaller distortive effect on behaviour. Indeed, taxes that are closely linked to local public good provision can be viewed to some degree as a payment for services. Empirically, recurrent taxes on immovable property have been found to be the least damaging tax to long-run economic growth, in comparison to consumption taxes, other property taxes, personal income taxes and corporate income taxes (OECD, 2010).

Taxes on financial and capital transactions are also in place in almost all OECD countries and generally account for a sizable portion of property tax revenues. These taxes, which include for instance stamp duties and financial transaction taxes, are in place in all but three OECD countries (Table 1.1). In 2015, they accounted on average for a little less than a quarter of total property tax revenues and 1.4% of total taxation in OECD countries. While these taxes are comparatively easy to collect, they can be highly distortive as they may prevent or limit transactions that would otherwise be mutually beneficial (Keen, 2014).

A majority of OECD countries also tax wealth transfers. 26 of the 35 OECD countries had taxes on wealth transfers in 2017 (see Table 1.1). The general trend for these taxes has been a move away from estate taxes which are levied on the deceased donor, towards inheritance and gift taxes that are levied on the beneficiaries (McDonnell, 2013).

However, revenues from inheritance or estate and gift taxes have been very low and declining over time. On average in the OECD, revenues from taxes on wealth transfers have been declining from 1.1% of total taxation in 1965 to 0.4% today (Figure 1.8). Low revenues reflect the fact that inheritance/estate and gift tax bases are often narrowed by numerous exemptions and deductions, and avoidance opportunities are widely available. The decline in tax revenues also reflects the fact that a number of countries have either abandoned or scaled back their wealth transfer taxes. However, differences across countries – and the higher revenues collected in Belgium and France, for instance (Figure 1.7) – suggest that the revenue potential of these taxes could be further exploited in many countries.

Interestingly, the mix of property tax instruments varies quite significantly across countries. Some countries levy a combination of many types of property taxes (e.g. Belgium, France, Italy, Spain, etc.) while others do not. For instance, two countries only levy recurrent taxes on immovable property (Estonia, Slovak Republic). There are also some countries which only tax wealth transfers and not total net wealth stocks; some countries which tax both; and others which tax neither including Australia, Czech Republic, Estonia, Israel, Mexico, New Zealand, the Slovak Republic and Sweden.

Table 1.1. Property taxes in place in OECD countries in 2017

Countries	Recurrent taxes on immovable property	Recurrent taxes on net wealth (individual and/or corporate)	Estate, inheritance and gift taxes	Taxes on financial and capital transactions	Non-recurrent taxes on property
Australia	V	x	x	V	x
Austria	V	x	V	V	V
Belgium	V	x	V	V	V
Canada	V	V	V	V	V
Chile	V	x	V	V	x
Czech Republic	V	x	x	V	x
Denmark	V	x	V	V	V
Estonia	V	x	x	x	x
Finland	V	x	V	V	x
France	V	V	V	V	x
Germany	V	x	V	V	x
Greece	V	x	V	V	x
Hungary	V	x	V	V	x
Iceland	V	x	V	V	V
Ireland	V	x	V	V	x
Israel	V	x	x	V	V
Italy	V	x	V	V	V
Japan	V	x	V	V	x
Korea	V	x	V	V	x
Latvia	V	x	V	V	x
Luxembourg	V	V	V	V	x
Mexico	V	x	x	V	x
Netherlands	V	x	V	V	x
New Zealand	V	x	x	V	x
Norway	V	V	x	V	x
Poland	V	x	V	V	x
Portugal	V	x	V	V	x
Slovak Republic	V	x	x	x	x
Slovenia	V	x	V	V	V
Spain	V	V	V	V	V
Sweden	V	x	x	V	x
Switzerland	V	V	V	V	x
Turkey	V	x	V	V	x
United Kingdom	V	x	V	V	V
United States	V	x	V	V	x

Source: IBFD Database

Overall, however, property tax revenues remain a small component of OECD countries' tax mixes. Property tax revenues accounted for less than 6% of the OECD's average tax mix in 2015. In comparison, SSCs, PIT and VAT respectively made up approximately 26%, 24% and 20% of OECD tax revenues on average. In addition, despite wealth growth in recent decades (Figure 1.6), the share of property tax revenues in the OECD's average tax mix has declined over time (Figure 1.8).

References

Iara, A. (2015), "Wealth Distribution and Taxation in EU Members", *Taxation Papers,* Working Paper No. 60, Brussels.

Hansson, A. (2010), "Is the Wealth Tax Harmful to Economic Growth?", *World Tax Journal*, Vol.10, No.1.

IMF (2014), "Fiscal Policy and Income Inequality", *IMF Policy Paper*, Washington, D.C.

Keen, M. (2014), "Taxing Wealth: Policy Challenges and Recent Debates", Presentation for the ECFIN Taxation Workshop - Taxing Wealth: Past, Present, Future, 13 November 2014.

Kopczuk, W. (2012), "Taxation of Intergenerational Transfers and Wealth", *NBER Working Paper Series*, No. 18584.

McDonnell, T.A. (2013), "Wealth Tax: Options for its Implementation in the Republic of Ireland", *NERI Working Paper Series*, WP 2013/6.

OECD (2017), *Revenue Statistics: 1965-2016*, OECD Publishing, Paris. http://dx.doi.org/10.1787/9789264283183-en

OECD (2010), *Tax Policy Reform and Economic Growth*, OECD Publishing, Paris. http://dx.doi.org/10.1787/9789264091085-en

Piketty, T., and G. Zucman (2013), "Capital is Back: Wealth-Income Ratios in Rich Countries 1700–2010", Paris School of Economics.

Chapter 2. Trends in the distribution of income and wealth

This chapter provides a brief overview of trends in the distribution of income and wealth in OECD countries. The chapter starts by looking at income inequality trends before examining trends in the distribution of wealth and patterns in the composition of assets across the wealth distribution.

The statistical data for Israel are supplied by and under the responsibility of the relevant Israeli authorities. The use of such data by the OECD is without prejudice to the status of the Golan Heights, East Jerusalem and Israeli settlements in the West Bank under the terms of international law.

This chapter provides a brief overview of trends in the distribution of income and wealth in the OECD. Patterns of asset holdings are critical to assessing the potential distributional effects of net wealth taxes. Trends in the distribution of income and wealth are also helpful to understand the renewed interest in net wealth taxes in recent years. This chapter starts by looking at income inequality trends in all OECD countries before examining trends in the distribution of wealth and patterns in the composition of assets across the wealth distribution.

Income inequality has increased in the last 30 years

Income inequality has increased in most OECD countries over the past three decades. The Gini coefficient of disposable income inequality stood at 0.29 on average across OECD countries in the mid-1980s. By 2013, it had increased by about 10% or 3 points to 0.32 (OECD, 2015). The latest available data shows that inequality has risen since the mid-1980s in 19 of the 22 OECD countries for which long-time series are available (Figure 2.1).

Nevertheless, trends in income inequality have varied across OECD countries. Inequality first started to rise in the late 1970s and early 1980s in some countries, notably English-speaking countries including the United Kingdom and the United States, as well as in Israel. From the late 1980s, the trend towards increasing disposable income inequality became more widespread, with widening income gaps not only in countries experiencing high levels of inequality but also in countries that were traditionally more equal such as Germany, Denmark and Sweden, where inequality rose faster than in any other OECD country in the 2000s (OECD, 2011). On the other hand, income inequality levels saw very little change in Belgium, France, Greece, Hungary and Mexico, and Turkey experienced a fall in inequality, which is consistent with trends in other emerging countries where inequality is very high but generally declining.

Figure 2.1. Disposable income Gini coefficients, mid-1980s and 2015 (or latest available year)

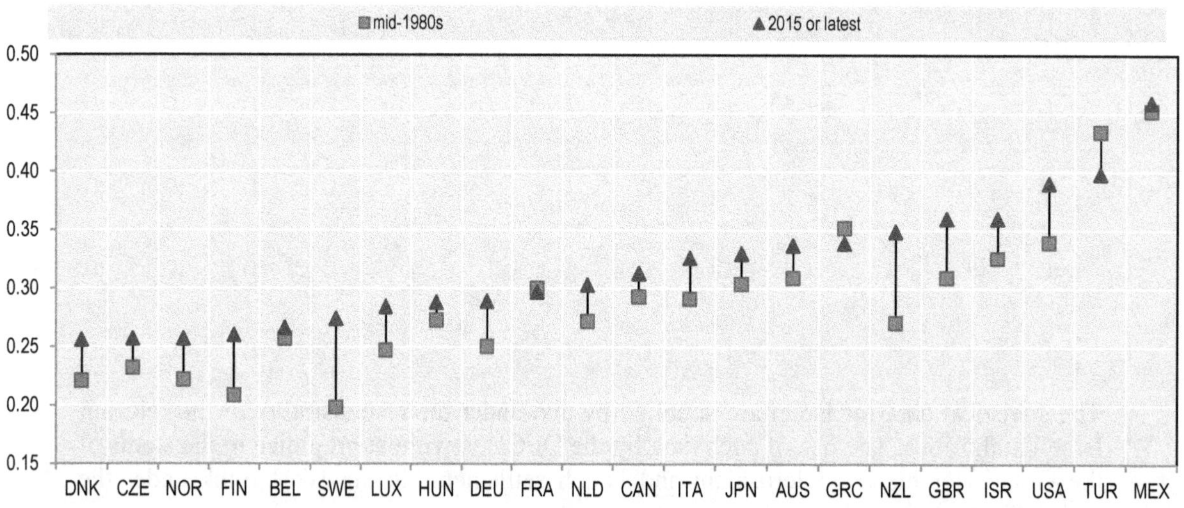

Source: OECD Income Distribution Database

In most OECD countries, the gap between the extremes of the income distribution has also reached its highest level since the early 1980s. In addition to increases in Gini coefficients which are more sensitive to changes in income shares in the middle than in the tails of the income distribution, inequality at the extremes of the income distribution has risen. The richest 10% of the population in the OECD now earn 9.5 times the income of the poorest 10%, compared to a ratio of 7:1 in the 1980s (Cingano, 2014).

The share of the top 1% of incomes in total income has also increased in most countries. According to the data shown in Figure 2.2, the rise was most remarkable in the United States. Top earners in other English-speaking countries also experienced a significant increase in their share of total income and the income shares of the top 1% increased by 70% and now reach about 7-8% in Finland, Norway and Sweden, which have traditionally been characterised by a more equal income distribution (Förster et al., 2014). By contrast, top earners' income shares grew much less in some of the continental European countries including France, the Netherlands and Spain.

However, some caution is necessary when considering measures of income inequality – with potential for both under- and over-estimation of levels and trends in income inequality. For example, some studies have suggested that commonly used data sources – including those cited above – underestimate the levels of income inequality by not accounting for tax evasion and avoidance, and by not valuing wealth held inside businesses (Piketty and Saez, 2006). Some studies suggest that tax evasion is higher for high income and high net wealth households than for lower income and net wealth households, meaning that a larger percentage of total income and wealth go unreported at the top of the income and net wealth distribution than at the bottom (Zucman, 2014). This suggests that when concealed wealth and income is taken into account, income and wealth inequality is even greater than the many existing estimates suggest. Finally, the choice of start and end points in such a comparison across time may also influence trends.[1]

In contrast, several studies, usually focusing on the United States, find lower levels and smaller increases in inequality (Auten and Splinter, 2017; Bricker et al., 2016; Burkhauser, et al., 2012). Looking at the United States, Auten and Splinter (2017) argue that measures based on tax returns are biased by tax bases changes and missing income sources. For instance, the income reported on tax returns has changed over time, in particular as a result of base broadening. Changes in reported income may also be the result of changes in tax incentives[2]. Besides, tax data misses important sources of income, including government transfer payments and non-taxable employer provided benefits. Finally, measures of long-term inequality may be affected by social changes, in particular declining marriage rates. When they account for these limitations, Auten and Splinter find that the increase in top 1% income shares decreases by two-thirds compared to the unadjusted measures of market income, used for example in Piketty and Saez (2003). Accounting for government transfers reduces the increase even more, by over 80%, and after-tax income results are similar.

Figure 2.2. Top 1% fiscal income share between 1980 and 2015 (or latest available year)

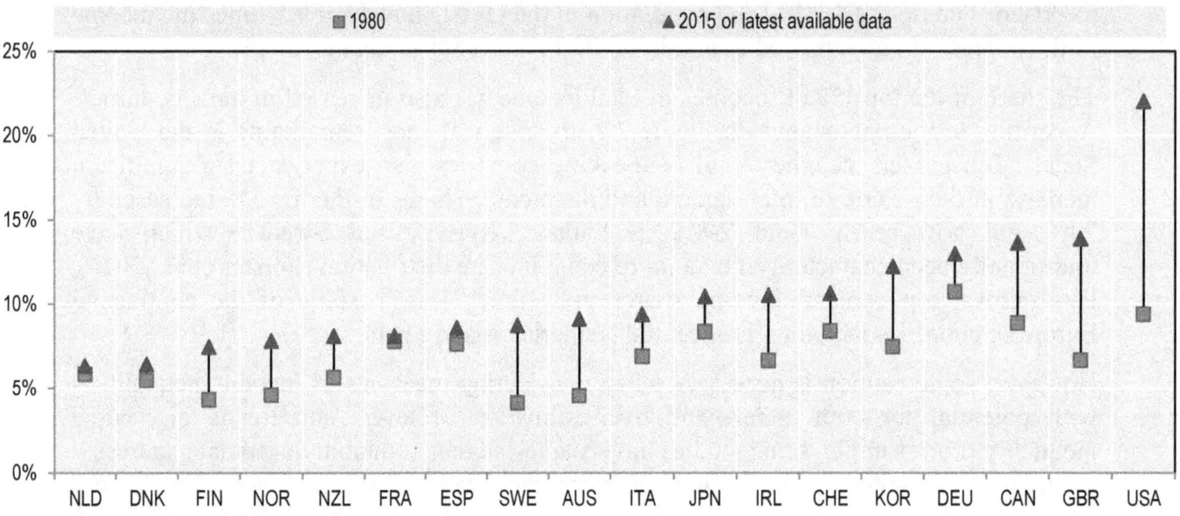

Source: World Wealth & Income Database

A distinguishing feature of top earners' income is the share of capital income in their total income. For the vast majority of individuals, wages are by far the largest component of income. Not surprisingly, however, the weight of wages tends to fall higher up the income ladder while the share of capital gains, capital income and business income increases (Förster et al., 2014). Nevertheless, patterns vary across countries. For instance, the top 0.01% receive about 20% of their income from capital in Canada while this share reaches almost 60% in France (OECD, 2014).

In the middle and at the bottom of the income distribution, on the other hand, there is evidence showing that incomes have either grown at a much lower pace or stagnated in a number of countries. For instance, the pre-tax incomes of middle-class households in the United States, the United Kingdom, and Japan have been found to have declined or stagnated in recent years (IMF, 2015). In the United States, Piketty, Saez and Zucman (2016) estimate that, between 1980 and 2013, average national income per adult grew by 60% in real terms across the economy, while national income per adult for the bottom 90% increased by only 30% and national income per adult for the bottom 50% has stagnated[3]. Data from the World Wealth and Income Database suggests that trends have varied across countries, however, with some countries, including France shown in the graph below, experiencing relatively stable income shares for the bottom 50% (Figure 2.3).

Figure 2.3. Bottom 50% income share in the United States and France

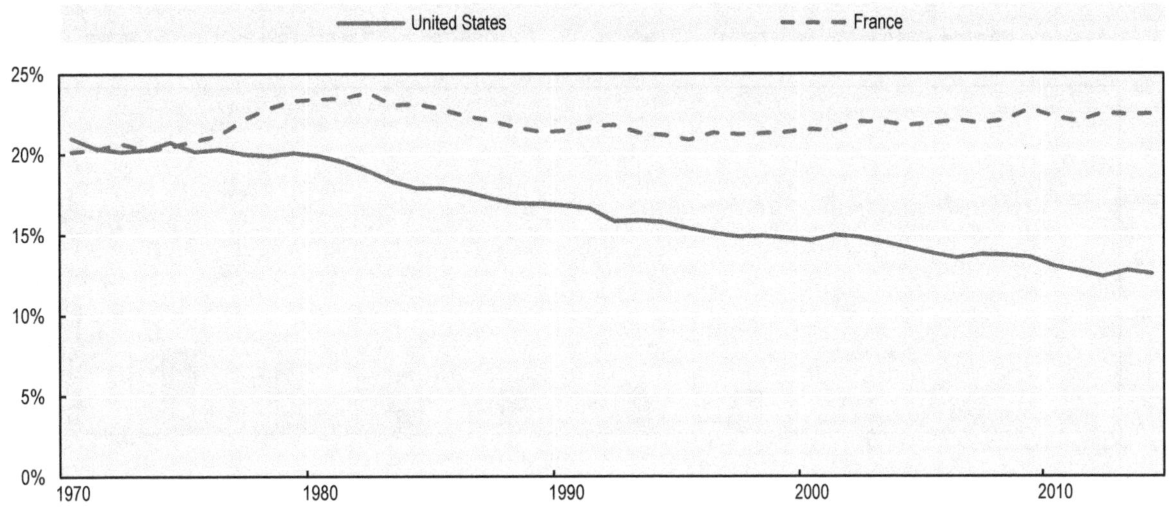

United States
France

25%
20%
15%
10%
5%
0%
1970
1980
1990
2000
2010

Source: World Wealth & Income Database

Increasing income inequality has been attributed to a range of factors including the globalisation and liberalisation of factor and product markets, skill-biased technological change and increasing firm concentration, which have contributed to a decline in the share of middle-skilled occupations relative to low- and high-skilled occupations and more generally to a decline in the labour share of income, i.e. the share of national income remunerating workers in the form of wages and benefits (Autor et al., 2017; IMF, 2017). Other explanatory factors for greater income inequality include the increasing bargaining power of high earners, changes in labour market institutions and regulations, declining top marginal income tax rates and more generally less progressive tax systems, as well as an increased concentration of assets (see below), which skews the distribution of capital income towards the top.

Wealth is more concentrated than income

Private wealth[4] is much more unequally distributed than income. In the 18 OECD countries for which comparable data is available, the bottom 40% own only 3% of total household wealth (Figure 2.4). In comparison, their share of total household income is 20%. At the other end of the spectrum, the top 10% of the wealth distribution hold half of total household wealth and the wealthiest 1% own almost a fifth. The wealth share of the top percentile in the wealth distribution is almost as large as the income share of the top decile in the income distribution (OECD, 2015). As shown in the graph below, wealth inequality is much greater than income inequality in part because many households do not have any (or sometimes even negative) wealth.

Figure 2.4. Distributions of household disposable income and net wealth across deciles

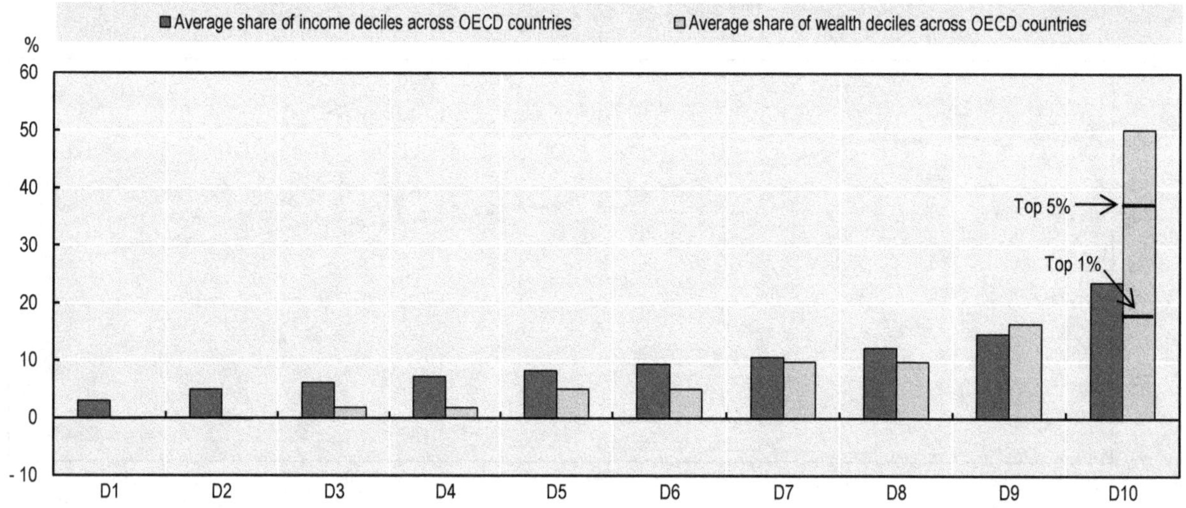

Note: OECD18 includes Australia, Austria, Belgium, Canada, Finland, France, Germany, Greece, Italy, Korea, Luxembourg, the Netherlands, Norway, Portugal, the Slovak Republic, Spain, the United Kingdom and the United States.
Source: OECD (2015) based on OECD Wealth Distribution Database and OECD Income Distribution Database

There is a strong but imperfect correlation between the distribution of income and wealth. A new OECD study on the taxation of household savings (OECD, 2018), based on household survey data for European countries, shows that those who earn a high income are also more likely to be wealthy, and those who earn a low income are more likely to have low levels of wealth. However, the correlation is by no means perfect. The association between income and wealth tends to be high at the two extremes of the distribution but much weaker in the middle: households at the bottom of the wealth distribution are more likely to be low-income households and high-wealth households are also usually high-income, while households in the middle of the wealth distribution tend to be more equally distributed along the income distribution (Durand and Murtin, 2015).

Box 2.1. Data sources to measure wealth concentration

Wealth tax declarations

The ideal source to measure wealth concentration would be high-quality wealth tax declarations for the entire population, with extensive and truthful reporting by both domestic and foreign financial institutions. No country in the world has such a perfect data source today. However, the countries that do have net wealth taxes generate useful data on wealth.

Estate and inheritance tax returns

Other tax data can be used to estimate wealth indirectly. A first approach is to use estate and inheritance tax returns to get information about wealth at death. From these sources one can infer how wealth is distributed across the living population, using the method known as the "mortal multiplier, which was invented before World War I by British and French economists.

Individual income tax returns

One can also use individual income tax returns and capitalise the dividends, interest, rents and other forms of capital income declared on such returns (see Saez and Zucman 2013 which uses the capitalisation technique to estimate the distribution of wealth annually in the United States since 1913).

Surveys

Wealth inequality can also be studied using surveys. In the United States, the Survey of Consumer Finances is available on a triennial basis from 1989 to 2013. In the euro area, the Household Finance and Consumption Survey (HFCS) provides harmonised micro-data on euro-area households' wealth and consumption. The key advantage of surveys is that they include detailed socio-demographic data and wealth questionnaires that allow the measurement of broad sets of assets for the entire population, including tax exempt assets and assets at the bottom of the wealth distribution that are not covered in tax data. Surveys have some important limitations, for instance, they are not available on a long-run basis and they raise serious difficulties regarding the measurement of wealth at the top of the distribution.

Source: Zucman (2016)

While it is very difficult to assess wealth distribution trends over time, some evidence points to increasing wealth inequality in recent decades. Piketty (2014) compiled data from eight OECD countries from the 1970s onwards and concluded that, like income, private wealth has tended to become more unequally distributed in recent decades. Several factors have contributed to this rise, most notably the increase in stock and housing prices relative to consumer prices. Saez and Zucman (2016) find evidence of greater wealth concentration in the United States where they estimate that the share of total household wealth owned by the top 0.1% increased from 7% in the late 1970s to 22% in 2012. Bricker et al. (2016), however, conclude that top wealth shares are lower and growing more slowly. For example, their preferred estimate is that the top 0.1%share increased from about 11% in 1992 to 15% in 2013.[5] Based on data from the World Wealth and Income Database, Figure 2.5 compares the evolution of the top 1% net personal wealth share in France, the United Kingdom and the United States, and confirms the trend towards greater wealth inequality in recent decades, in particular in the United States, reversing a long-term decline throughout much of the 20th century.

Figure 2.5. Top 1% net personal wealth share in France, the United Kingdom and the United States

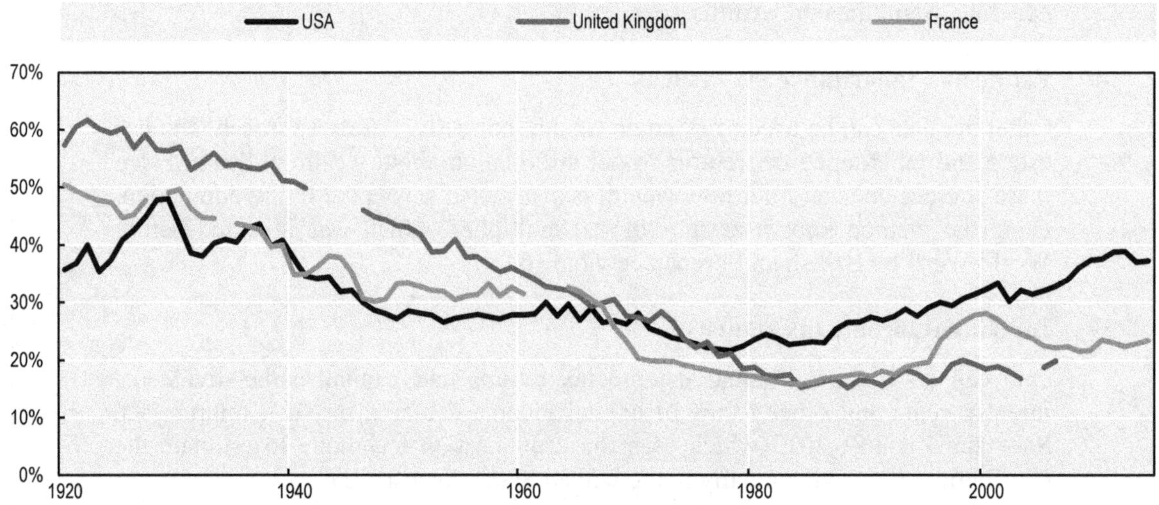

Source: World Wealth & Income Database

There is also some indication that, since the crisis, trends towards greater wealth inequality have continued. Comparable data for six OECD countries (Australia, Canada, Italy, the Netherlands, the United Kingdom and the United States) indicates that, since the crisis, wealth concentration at the top has increased in four of them (Italy, the Netherlands, the United States and the United Kingdom), while wealth inequality at the bottom of the distribution increased in all countries except the United Kingdom (OECD, 2015).

The composition of wealth varies with taxpayers' levels of wealth

With regard to the composition of assets, overall, households hold the largest share of their wealth in the form of real assets, though this is less pronounced at high wealth levels. Survey data suggests that non-financial assets represent between 70% and 90% of total household wealth in developed countries (IMF, 2014). It is only at the top of the wealth distribution that financial assets start representing a significant source of wealth (OECD, 2015). As shown in Figure 2.6, while non-financial assets are still the largest component of wealth for the fifth quintile, financial assets represent on average about a third of net wealth in the 18 countries for which data is available.

Figure 2.6. Wealth composition and average net wealth by quintile for 18 OECD countries

2010 or latest available year, values in 2005 USD

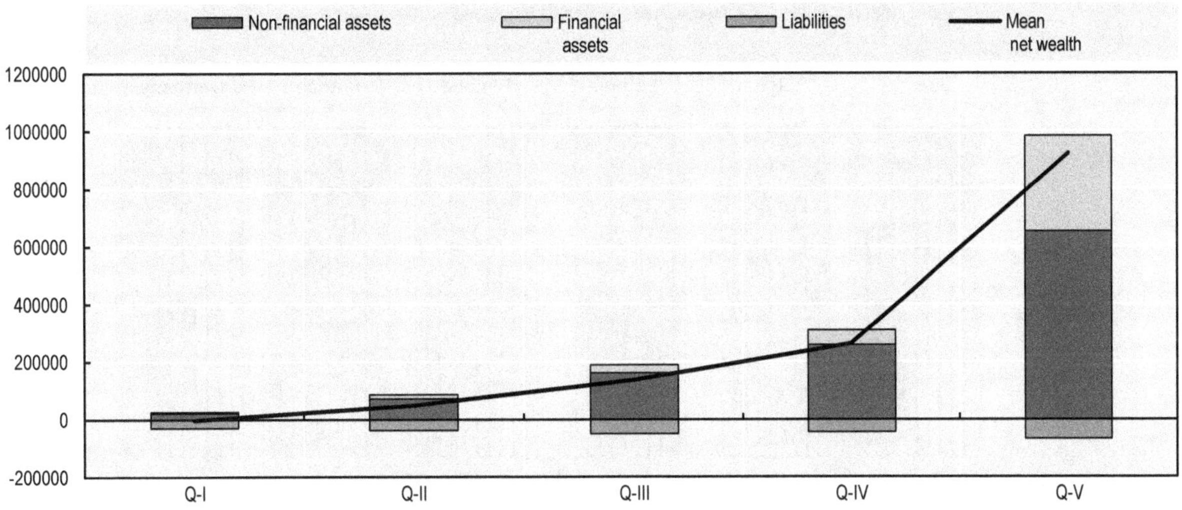

Note: OECD18 includes Australia, Austria, Belgium, Canada, Finland, France, Germany, Greece, Italy, Korea, Luxembourg, the Netherlands, Norway, Portugal, the Slovak Republic, Spain, the United Kingdom and the United States.
Source: OECD (2015) based OECD Wealth Distribution Database

Among real assets (and indeed overall), the main residence is predominant. Figure 2.7 comes from a new OECD study on the taxation of household savings (OECD, 2018) and is based on data from the Eurosystem Household Finance and Consumption Survey (HFCS). It shows that the main residence makes up the largest share of real assets among the middle net wealth deciles and that this pattern is relatively consistent across countries. For lower net wealth deciles, housing forms a slightly lower share of gross assets. Regarding vehicles and valuables, their share varies widely across net wealth deciles, but on average they make up a small share of wealth for top deciles in all countries and substantial shares of those with low levels of wealth. At the top, large shares of real assets are held in the form of second (or third or fourth) residences. Households in top net wealth deciles also have high shares of gross wealth held in the form of self-employed businesses. This reduces the share of total assets held in the main residence, especially in the top wealth decile.

Figure 2.7. Breakdown of real assets, as a share of total real assets, by net wealth deciles

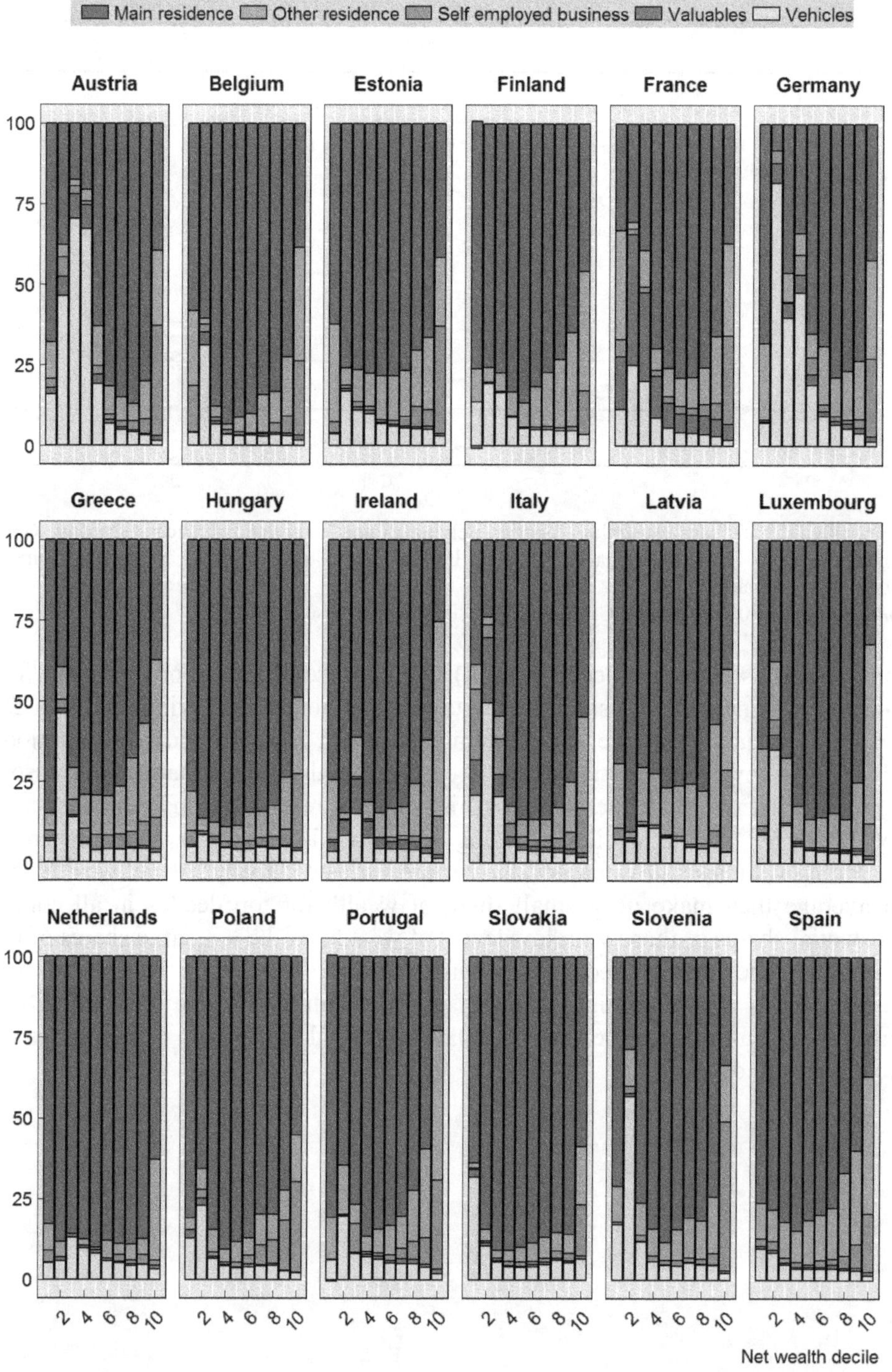

Note: Data are for 2013-14

Source: *OECD Taxation of Household Savings* (OECD, 2018) *based* on Household Finance and Consumption Survey (2017).

With regard to financial assets, their distribution and composition vary across wealth deciles. As mentioned above, financial assets are held mostly by those with higher levels of net wealth. However, they also make up a large share of total wealth for those at the very bottom of the net wealth distribution, mainly because those at the bottom of the net wealth distribution have very low levels of net housing wealth. Caution should be taken in interpreting survey data estimates of asset holdings, however, as they rely on what households declare to statistical agencies. This is particularly true for financial assets for which, in addition to inaccuracies, underreporting behaviours may be common.

Bank deposits are the most common financial assets, although less so at the top of the wealth distribution. Overall, bank deposits account for a substantial share of households' total financial assets. Figure 2.8 shows variations across net wealth deciles. Bank deposits make up a much smaller share of the asset mix for those at the top of the net wealth distribution. They account for 42.4% of gross financial asset holdings on average for those in the highest net wealth decile. Households in these higher net wealth deciles are more likely to hold financial assets in other forms relative to those in lower net wealth deciles. In contrast, bank deposits comprise 52.4% of gross financial asset holdings on average for households in the lowest net wealth decile. These variations in bank deposits in part reflect different levels of risk aversion, with wealthy individuals allocating a much larger share of their financial portfolios to risky assets (Bach et al., 2015). These savings choices may also be driven in part by varying levels of financial sophistication, with low-income and low-net wealth taxpayers choosing to save in bank deposits because of a lack of financial literacy and knowledge about saving opportunities with higher returns.

Holdings of shares and bonds are concentrated at the top of the net wealth distribution. Households in the top net wealth decile hold 7.4% of all financial assets in the form of shares, while households in the bottom net wealth decile hold only 1.3% on average. Households in the top net wealth decile hold 5.3% of all financial assets in the form of bonds, while households in the bottom net wealth decile hold 0.4%. The average across all net wealth deciles is 1.9%.

In many countries, individuals engage in substantial private pension savings, which is a source of variation in asset holdings across wealth and age levels. Pension savings are a widely used form of saving that usually forms the second largest share of financial assets held in HFCS countries, after bank deposits. Holdings of pension wealth generally decrease along the net wealth distribution as a share of total holdings, though modestly. In the top net wealth decile, households hold on average 16.9% of all financial assets in the form of pension savings, while households in the bottom net wealth decile hold 31.8%. The average across all net wealth deciles is 22.8%.

There is nevertheless substantial variation in the mix of financial assets held across countries. This is particularly the case for pension savings. For instance, Ireland exhibits very high shares of pension wealth (59% of total gross financial wealth on average), but comparatively low shares of wealth held in the form of bank deposits. On the other hand, in Greece, bank deposits account for the vast majority of wealth, including at the top of the wealth distribution, with very little wealth held in the form of pension savings. Estonia and Latvia are also characterised by low levels of wealth held in the form of pension savings. Assets in mutual funds and managed accounts represent relatively significant shares of total assets in top net wealth deciles in Belgium, Finland, Hungary, Italy and Luxembourg.

Overall, many factors account for cross-country differences in the composition of wealth. For instance, the share of financial assets compared to real assets tends to be higher in countries with large private pension systems, high levels of financial development and greater levels of financial education. The share of financial assets may also be higher in countries that have large public housing sectors which tend to discourage home ownership (IMF, 2014). Trends in asset values are also a major factor affecting the composition of wealth. Finally, differences in taxation may influence the composition of household assets.

Figure 2.8. Breakdown of financial assets, as a share of total financial assets, by net wealth deciles

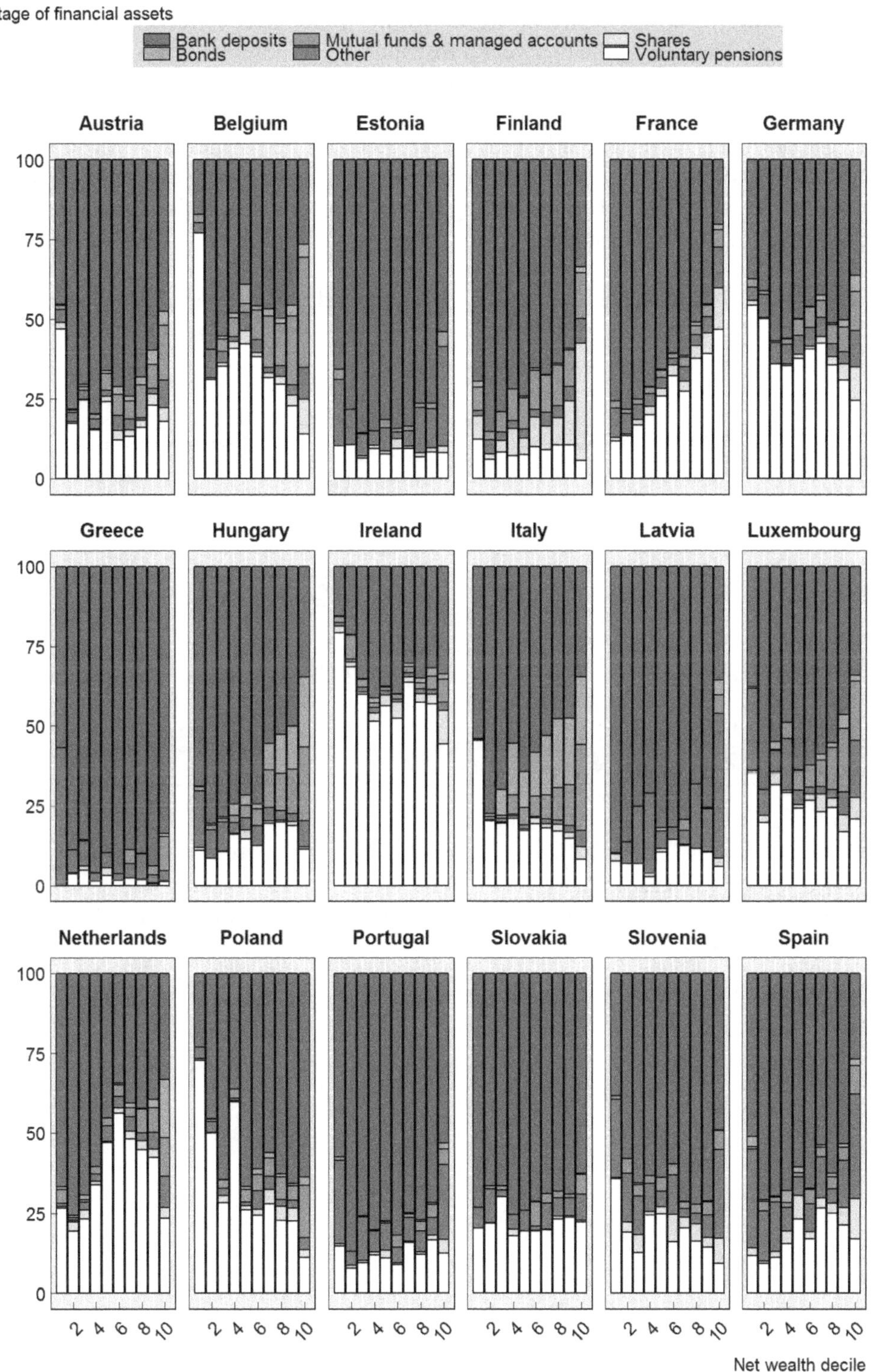

Note: Data are for 2013-14

Source: *OECD Taxation of Household Savings* (OECD, 2018) *based* on Household Finance and Consumption Survey (2017).

Poor households have greater levels of debt relative to their wealth. As a share of gross wealth, those in low net wealth deciles have much higher levels of debt than those in high net wealth deciles. Figure 2.9 shows that the average amount of household debt as a share of gross wealth is much higher in the lowest net wealth decile than for any other decile and that it declines along the net wealth distribution. In nominal terms, and looking at the distribution of household debt across income deciles, however, Figure 2.10 shows that borrowing increases when income increases. Thus, debt deductibility or deductions for interest payments will generally provide greater nominal benefits to those with higher incomes but will also provide higher proportional benefits to those with low levels of net wealth. Figures 2.9 and 2.10 also highlights that most household liabilities are mortgages on the purchase of main residences.

Figure 2.9. Household debt as a share of gross wealth, by income and net wealth deciles

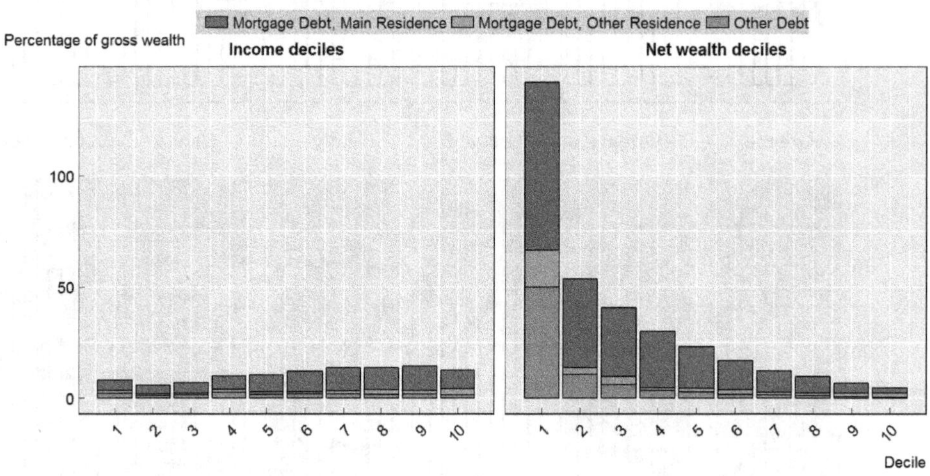

Note: Data are for 2013-14 (see Box 1).
Source: *OECD Taxation of Household Savings* (OECD, 2018) *based* on Household Finance and Consumption Survey (2017).

Figure 2.10. Household debt in EUR, by income and net wealth deciles

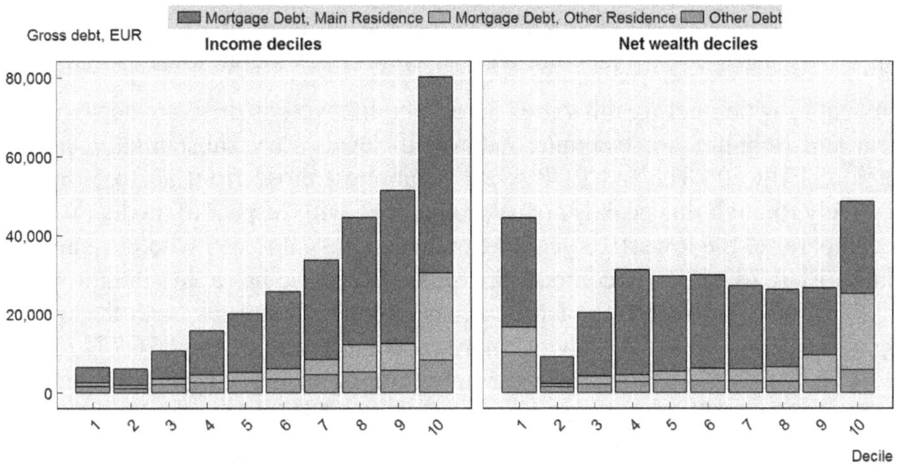

Note: Data are for 2013-14 (see Box 1).
Source: *OECD Taxation of Household Savings* (OECD, 2018) based on Household Finance and Consumption Survey (2017).

Some evidence shows that increasing indebtedness at the bottom of the wealth distribution has been an important driver of wealth inequality in some countries. In the United States, growing indebtedness has been a major factor behind the erosion of the wealth share of the bottom 90%. For a long time, rising indebtedness was compensated by increases in the values of assets held by the middle class but this trend came to an end with the crisis (Saez and Zucman, 2016). This suggests that correcting wealth inequality cannot only be achieved by curbing wealth accumulation at the top but also requires stimulating the accumulation of wealth at the bottom of the wealth and income distribution.

Wealth holdings generally follow a lifecycle pattern

The net wealth of households varies over time. The within-decile distribution of net wealth is a snapshot in time. As individuals enter the workforce, their income and net wealth are both likely to begin to rise compared to childhood. As individuals retire, their incomes often fall substantially, and their net wealth may decline as they dis-save over their retirement years (though this dis-saving may not apply to households with the highest levels of wealth). These trends may be masked if the income and net wealth distributions are examined without taking age into account.

On average, household net wealth is highest in the years just before retirement. Figure 2.11 shows average and median net wealth across the age distribution. Overall, net wealth is highest amongst those from 50-59 years old, with an average net wealth level of EUR 205 501, and lowest amongst those from 20-29 years old, with an average net wealth level of EUR 68 600. The top three net wealth age groups are ages 50-59 years old, 40-49 years old and 60-69 years old, where the latter two groups have average net wealth levels of EUR 158 082 and EUR 222 938 respectively.

Median wealth across age groups is lower than average wealth across age group, which stems from the relatively high concentration of wealth at the top of the net wealth distribution. However, the stylised patterns across ages are similar to the patterns with respect to average wealth levels across age groups. Overall, net wealth is highest amongst those aged 60-69 years old, with a median net wealth level of EUR 222 128, and lowest amongst those aged 20-29 years old, with an average net wealth level of EUR 47 727.

The extent to which net wealth varies across the lifecycle is different across countries. In Austria and Belgium, for example, net wealth levels vary substantially, peaking at an average of EUR 506 811 and EUR 492 371 amongst those from 50 to 59 and 60 to 69 respectively (though this peak is not as pronounced with respect to median wealth levels). This compares to the lowest 10-year age bracket (ages 20 to 29) who have an average net wealth of EUR 282 329. By contrast, the Slovak Republic has a distribution of net wealth that is relatively flat in absolute terms across various age groups, with the wealthiest age group – those from 50 to 59 – having an average net wealth of EUR 76 772 (and a median level of EUR 61 474) compared to the age group with the lowest average net wealth - those from 20 to 29, who have a net wealth of EUR 22 165 (and a median level of EUR 8 777). This may suggest low levels of aggregate household savings for retirement. These results should be considered with caution, however, given that the estimates of pension wealth in the HFSC are not comprehensive (for more information, see the OECD's 2018 study on the Taxation of Household Savings).

Figure 2.11. Net wealth across the age distribution, EUR

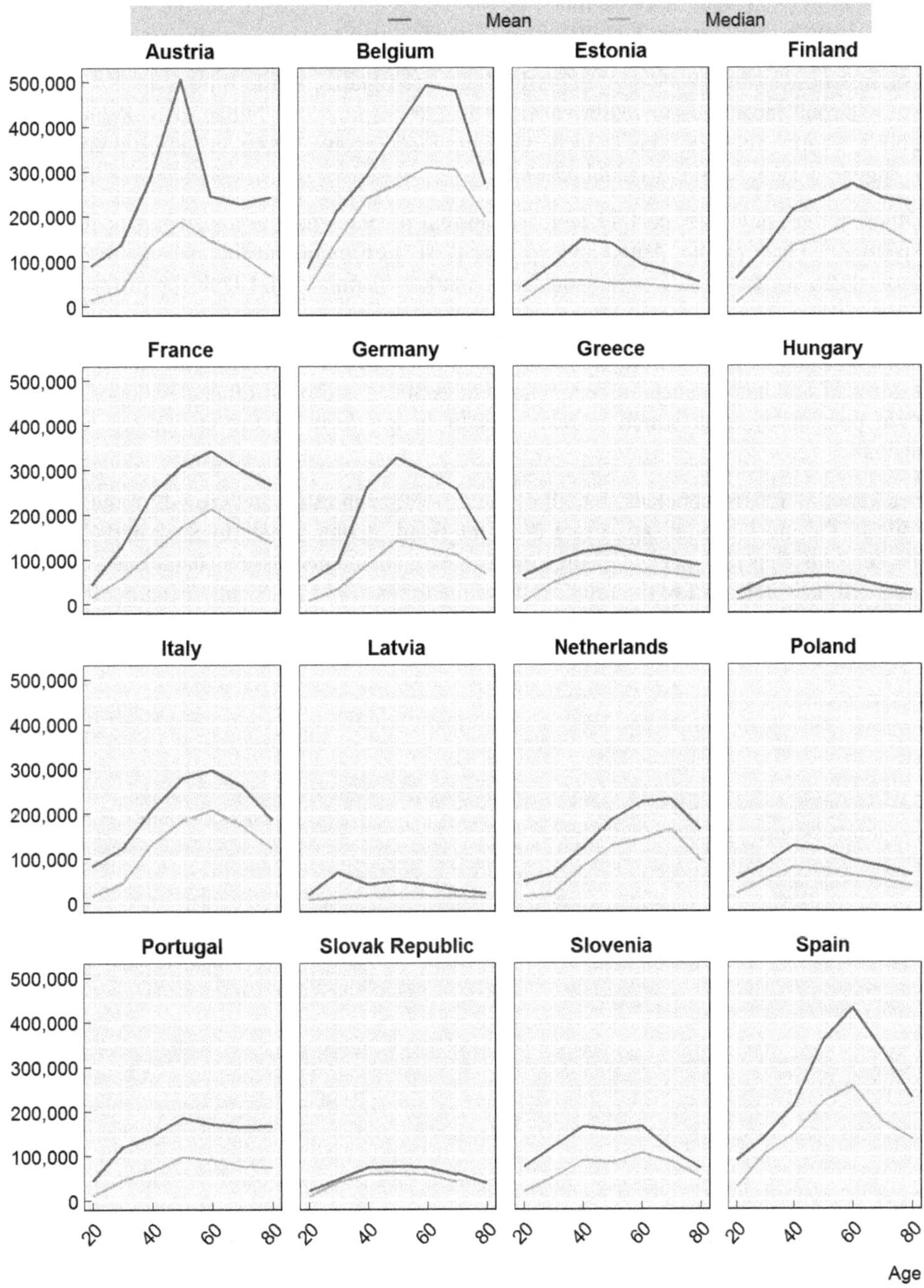

Note: Data are for 2013-14 (see Box 1).
Source: *OECD Taxation of Household Savings* (OECD, 2018) based on Household Finance and Consumption Survey (2017).

Notes

[1] For example, while survey data for New Zealand shows a higher disposable income Gini coefficient in 2013 than in 1984, much of the increase occurred in the late 1980s – such that the Gini is lower in 2013 than in 1993 (Ball and Creedy, 2016).

[2] For instance, in the 1960s and 1970s in the United States, top PIT rates of 70% gave business owners strong incentives to retain earnings inside corporations rather than paying dividends or higher executive salaries. This reduced measured top income shares because retained earnings do not appear as income on individual returns.

[3] Other studies, however, do find increases in real incomes for the lower part of the U.S. income distribution. For example, Auten and Splinter (2017) estimate that the average real income of the bottom 90% increased 127% for consistent market income and 172% for pre-tax income from 1979 to 2015.

[4] It is important to note that the commonly used measures of wealth only include private wealth in the form of real and financial assets. The United States and most other developed countries have public pension systems which provide wealth in the form of the capitalised value of future pensions.

[5] Bricker et al. (2016) conclude that all of the difference in estimated growth of the top 0.1% share is due to the gross capitalisation rate used for fixed income assets in Saez and Zucman (2016). This capitalisation rate generated the result that fixed income assets (bank accounts and bonds) accounted for nearly half of the total assets of the top 0.1% in 2013 and virtually all of the increase in the top 0.1% share between 2001 and 2013.

References

Auten, G. and D. Splinter (2017) "Income inequality in the United States: Using tax data to measure long-term trends", US Treasury Department and Joint Committee on Taxation (unpublished paper).

Autor, D., Dorn, D., Katz, L.F., Patterson, C. and J. Van Reenen (2017), "The Fall of the Labor Share and the Rise of Superstar Firms", NBER Working Paper, No. 23396.

Bach, L, Calvet, L. E. and P. Sodini (2017), "Rich pickings? Risk, return, and skill in the portfolios of the wealthy" CEPR Discussion Paper, No. 11734.

Ball, C. and J. Creedy (2016) "Inequality in New Zealand 1983/84 to 2012/13", New Zealand Economic Papers, Vol. 50, No. 3, pp. 323-342.

Bricker, J., Henriques, A., Krimmel, J. and J. Sabelhaus (2016), "Measuring Income and Wealth at the Top Using Administrative and Survey Data", Brookings Papers on Economic Activity Spring, pp. 261-312.

Burkhauser, R. V., Feng, S., Jenkins, S. P. and J. Larrimore (2012), "Recent Trends in Top Income Shares in the United States: Reconciling Estimates from March CPS and IRS Tax Return Data", The Review of Economics and Statistics, Vol. 44, No. 2, pp. 371-388.

Cingano, F. (2014), "Trends in Income Inequality and its Impact on Economic Growth", OECD Social, Employment and Migration Working Papers, No. 163, OECD Publishing, Paris. http://dx.doi.org/10.1787/1815199X

Durand, M. and F. Murtin (2016), "The Relationship between Income and Wealth Inequality: Evidence from the New OECD Wealth Distribution Database", paper prepared for the IARIW Sessions at the 2015 World Statistics Conference Sponsored by the International Statistical Institute.

Förster,M., Llena-Nozal, A. and V. Nafilyan (2014), "Trends in Top Incomes and their Taxation in OECD Countries", OECD Social, Employment and Migration Working Papers, No. 159, OECD Publishing, Paris.

IMF (2017), "Chapter 3: Understanding the Downward Trend in Labour Income Shares", in World Economic Outlook, April 2017: Gaining Momentum?, Washington, D.C.

IMF (2015), "Fiscal Policy and Long-Term Growth", IMF Policy Paper, Washington, D.C.

IMF (2014), "Fiscal Policy and Income Inequality", IMF Policy Paper, Washington, D.C.

Kopczuk, W., Martin J., and K. Telle (2016), "Accounting for Business Income in Measuring Top Income Shares: Integrated Accrual Approach Using Individual and Firm Data from Norway", available at http://www.columbia.edu/~wk2110/papers.html

OECD (2018), Taxation of Household Savings, Tax Policy Studies, OECD Publishing, Paris. http://dx.doi.org/10.1787/19900538

OECD (2015), In It Together: Why Less Inequality Benefits All, OECD Publishing, Paris. http://dx.doi.org/10.1787/9789264235120-en

OECD (2014a), "Focus on Top Incomes and Taxation in OECD Countries: Was the crisis a game changer?", OECD, Paris.

OECD (2011), Divided We Stand: Why Inequality Keeps Rising, OECD Publishing, Paris. http://dx.doi.org/10.1787/9789264119536-en

Piketty, T. (2014), Capital in the Twenty-First Century, Harvard University Press.

Piketty, T. and E. Saez (2006), "The Evolution of Top Incomes: A Historical and International Perspective", American Economic Review, Papers and Proceedings, Vol. 96, No. 2, pp. 200-205.

Piketty, T. and E. Saez (2003), "Income Inequality in the United States, 1913-1998," Quarterly Journal of Economics, Vol. 118, No. 1, pp. 1-39.

Piketty, T., Saez, E. and G. Zucman (2016), "Distributional National Accounts: Methods and Estimates for the United States", NBER Working Paper, No. 22945.

Saez, E. and G. Zucman (2016), "Wealth Inequality in the United States since 1913: Evidence from Capitalized Income Tax Data", Quarterly Journal of Economics, Vol. 131, No. 2.

Zucman, G. (2016), "Wealth Inequality", State of the Union: The Poverty and Inequality Report, Pathways, Special Issue 2016, Stanford Center on Poverty and Inequality.

Chapter 3. The case for and against individual net wealth taxes

This chapter reviews the arguments for and against individual net wealth taxes. These arguments relate to the efficiency, equity and administrative implications of net wealth taxes. The effects of capital income taxes and taxes on wealth transfers are also discussed to examine how these taxes interact with net wealth taxes and whether they can be complements or substitutes to taxes on net wealth.

This chapter is based on the tax rules that were in place as of 1 September 2017. Since then, France has replaced its net wealth tax ("*impôt de solidarité sur la fortune*") with a new real estate wealth tax ("*impôt sur la fortune immobilière*"), with effect from 1 January 2018.

This chapter is a review of the arguments both for and against individual net wealth taxes. The chapter discusses these arguments and assesses their validity. These arguments relate to the efficiency, equity and administrative implications of net wealth taxes. The effects of capital income taxes and taxes on wealth transfers will also be discussed to examine how these taxes interact with net wealth taxes and whether they can be complements or substitutes to taxes on net wealth. Overall, this chapter concludes that, both from an efficiency and equity perspective, there are limited arguments for having a net wealth tax on top of well-designed capital income taxes – including taxes on capital gains – and inheritance taxes, but that there are stronger arguments for having a net wealth tax as an (imperfect) substitute for these taxes.

Characteristics of net wealth taxes

Capital is typically taxed through both income and property taxes (Table 3.1). Capital income taxes are levied on the flow of income from assets. Property taxes, on the other hand, are levied on assets. Property taxes can be subdivided into two major categories of taxes – taxes on the transfers of property and taxes on the use and ownership of taxes. In this section, net wealth taxes, which are defined as recurrent taxes on individuals' net wealth stocks, will be contrasted with both taxes on personal capital income and other types of property taxes. It should be mentioned, however, that capital income can also be taxed through social security contributions, as has been the case in France with the "*contribution sociale généralisée*" and that the boundary between capital income taxes and property taxes may sometimes be blurry as, for instance, taxes on immovable property levied on the basis of a presumptive net income and which take into account taxpayers' personal circumstances, are classified as income taxes under the OECD's *Revenue Statistics* classification (OECD, 2016).

Table 3.1. A typology of taxes on capital

Type of tax		Examples
Taxes on capital income		Corporate income taxes Personal capital income taxes (on interest, dividends, rents, capital gains)
Property taxes	Taxes on property transfers	Inheritance/estate and gift taxes Taxes on financial and capital transactions
	Taxes on the use and ownership of property	Recurrent taxes on immovable property Recurrent taxes on individual net wealth Recurrent taxes on businesses' net assets Non-recurrent taxes on property (e.g. sporadic capital levies)

Source: Authors.

Comparing net wealth tax with personal capital income taxes

There are similarities between the taxation of net wealth and the taxation of capital income. For instance, if an individual taxpayer has a total net wealth of EUR 10 million that earns a rate of return of 4% (or a return of EUR 400 000), the tax liability will be the same whether the government levies a tax of 30% on the capital income of EUR 400 000 (EUR 120 000) or a wealth tax of 1.2% on the capital stock of EUR 10 million. This means that a capital income tax of 30% would equate to a wealth tax of 1.2% where the rate of return is 4%.

A key difference, however, is that a net wealth tax is imposed irrespective of actual returns. Net wealth taxes do not tax the actual return earned on assets but are equivalent to the taxation of a presumptive (i.e. fixed) return. This implies that, as opposed to a capital income tax, a net wealth tax implicitly imposes a lower effective tax on the return of high-yield assets compared to low-yield assets. Using the example above, if the return increases to 5%, the capital income tax liability will increase to EUR 150 000, while the wealth tax liability will remain the same, implying a drop in the effective tax on the return. This feature of wealth taxation is central to any discussion concerning its equity and efficiency effects.

A net wealth tax can be more comprehensive than a capital income tax. As opposed to capital income taxes, under a net wealth tax, even the assets that do not generate monetary returns are generally taxed. For instance, artworks that increase their owner's wellbeing but do not generate any monetary returns until they are sold are often (at least partly) included in the tax base. Assets that generate returns that are not readily observable (e.g. owner-occupied housing generating an imputed return) are also taxed.

A third key difference is that a wealth tax is in theory levied on an accrual basis. Indeed, under the assumption that the wealth tax base is kept up to date through regular asset valuations, the appreciation in asset values is taxed every year under a wealth tax. On the other hand, under income taxation, taxes are levied on a realisation basis, meaning that taxes are levied when assets are sold on the increase in value between the time they were purchased and sold. In theory, it would be possible to tax capital gains on an accrual-equivalent basis but this has very rarely been implemented in practice. Accrual-based taxation has a number of advantages: it does not create lock-in effects and the resulting inefficiencies in capital allocation and it enhances fairness as appreciations in asset values are a better reflection of taxpayers' current wealth. However, taxation on an accrual basis involves numerous practical difficulties, and if asset values are not regularly updated, the wealth tax becomes more comparable to a tax on a realisation basis.

Another major difference between the taxation of capital income and the taxation of wealth is related to their capacity to raise revenues in a volatile economic environment. If capital income is equal to zero or negative, the tax liability will also be zero under a capital income tax, while it will still be positive under a wealth tax if the capital value of the assets remains positive. As a result, net wealth taxes are a more stable tax revenue source than capital income taxes but they differ in their automatic stabilisation properties (Keen, 2014), which may have consequences on entrepreneurship and risk-taking as discussed below.

Interaction between capital income tax rates and the net wealth tax base

Taxes on capital income reduce the net expected return on the existing capital stock and therefore reduce the value of the assets in which the tax rate has been capitalised. For instance, the value of corporate shares reflects the net present value of the after-tax dividends to which the share owners are entitled. An increase in the taxes on dividend income will therefore lower the value of those shares, at least in the short run when firms cannot change their capital stock and investment behaviour in response to the tax increase (see also the discussion on the different views of dividend taxation in OECD, 2007). The more inelastic the supply of capital, the larger the extent to which taxes will be capitalised into asset prices. As immovable property is typically inelastic in supply, changes in the tax rates levied on housing will generally have a strong impact on house prices.

The capitalisation of taxes creates some interdependence between the taxes on capital income and the net wealth tax. An increase in taxes on personal capital income will reduce the value of income-generating assets. An increase in capital income taxes will therefore result in a smaller net wealth tax base, and potentially in a reduction in wealth tax revenues.

Similarly, a reduction in capital income taxes can be expected to increase asset values, generating windfall gains for existing asset owners, on the one hand, and increasing the net wealth tax base, on the other hand. This applies to mortgage interest relief as well. Mortgage interest relief lowers the income tax liability but may also increase the value of immovable property which, if housing is included in the tax base, will broaden the net wealth tax base. Depending on the design of the tax relief and the income and wealth taxes, the income tax advantage that high-wealth taxpayers obtain might be neutralised, to some extent, by the increase in wealth taxes as a result of the increase in housing prices. Whether the negative impact on income tax revenues of a capital income tax reduction will outweigh the positive impact on net wealth tax revenues when asset prices increase will depend on the design of income and wealth taxes in general, and on the degree of tax capitalisation and the level of the wealth tax rate in particular.

These observations not only apply to income taxes but also apply to the impact of the wealth tax itself. An increase in the wealth tax rate, for instance, will decrease the value of the assets whose price is predominantly set by individuals who are subject to the net wealth tax in that jurisdiction, thereby narrowing the net wealth tax base. The wealth tax is likely to affect its own tax base through tax capitalisation.

Comparing net wealth taxes with other taxes on personal property

Property taxes cover a wide variety of taxes levied on the ownership, transfer or use of property. According to the OECD Revenue Statistics classification (OECD, 2017), they include recurrent taxes on immovable property, which can be levied on property owners, tenants or both; recurrent taxes on net wealth, which include both individual and corporate taxes; estate, inheritance and gift taxes; taxes on financial and capital transactions; and non-recurrent taxes on property. These taxes have different goals as well as different effects in terms of revenue, efficiency, equity and tax administration. In practice, the mix of property tax instruments used by countries varies across the OECD (see Chapter 1).

As opposed to other taxes on wealth holdings, in particular recurrent taxes on immovable property, net wealth taxes are levied on a broad range of capital stock or property. Net wealth taxes are levied on immovable property, movable assets and financial investments. The main rationale is that total wealth stocks are a better reflection of taxpayers' ability to pay. In addition, as financial assets make up a large share of wealth at the top of the wealth distribution, taxing total wealth is more progressive than taxing exclusively immovable property. However, a net wealth tax involves more practical challenges, largely because of the mobility of financial assets and the difficulty associated with valuing some categories of infrequently traded assets.

In contrast with sporadic capital levies or taxes on the transfer of capital, net wealth taxes are levied on a regular basis (usually annually). A sporadic capital levy has attractive features as a revenue raising instrument because it is a lump sum tax. This means that it taxes past wealth already accumulated, and therefore should not cause any distortions. While there are good arguments for such a tax, there have been in practice few successful examples of such taxes (Keen, 2014). Inheritance or estate taxes are also only levied once either on the deceased donor or on the recipient(s).

As opposed to inheritance taxes, wealth taxes are levied on both inherited and self-made wealth. Under a net wealth tax, there is no distinction between wealth resulting from personal effort and lifetime savings, inherited wealth, increases in asset values or luck (e.g. lottery). As discussed below, there may be both equity and efficiency justifications for taxing different sources of wealth differently.

Similar to inheritance or estate taxes, however, wealth taxes are imposed on net assets, meaning that debts are deductible. Net assets are a closer reflection of taxpayers' ability to pay than gross wealth. They differ in this regard from recurrent taxes on immovable property, which are measured gross of debt. Not allowing for debt deductibility under recurrent taxes on immovable property may limit highly leveraged housing investment and the accumulation of high household debts but may raise distributional concerns: two taxpayers who own property of comparable value but with different levels of debt will pay the same amount of property tax. What countries do instead is to provide mortgage interest relief from PIT.

The case for net wealth taxes

This section reviews the arguments in favour of net wealth taxes. Arguments in favour of net wealth taxes broadly fall into two categories: (1) arguments for having a wealth tax *on top of* capital income taxes and other taxes on property and (2) arguments for having a wealth tax as a *substitute* for taxes on capital or capital income. This section reviews both sets of arguments.

Reducing wealth inequality and promoting equality of opportunity

As discussed in Chapter 2, private wealth is much more unequally distributed than income and there is some evidence suggesting that wealth inequality has increased in recent decades. While it is very difficult to assess wealth distribution trends over time, some studies point to increasing wealth inequality in recent decades. For instance, Piketty (2014) compiled data from eight OECD countries since the 1970s and concluded that, like income, private wealth has tended to become more unequally distributed in recent decades, reversing a long-term decline throughout much of the 20th century. Evidence of greater wealth concentration is particularly strong in the United States where Saez and Zucman (2016) find for instance that the share of total household wealth owned by the top 0.1% increased from 7% in the late 1970s to 22% in 2012. Bricker et al., estimated that the increase was from 11% to 15% (see Chapter 2).

These recent wealth distribution trends have strengthened the distributional case for taxing net wealth. Indeed, because wealth is highly concentrated at the top of the wealth distribution, even a low proportional tax on wealth holdings can increase progressivity. In a few OECD countries – in particular Nordic countries – which tax personal capital income at a flat rate, wealth taxes have been justified as a way of adding progressivity to the taxation of capital (Silfverberg, 2002). Data for Norway shows that the net wealth tax makes the overall tax system progressive at the top of the income distribution (Norwegian Ministry of Finance, 2017). Also as a consequence of the high concentration of wealth at the top and the large amount of private wealth, in theory even a low tax with a high exemption threshold excluding the lifecycle savings of most taxpayers could still raise a sizeable amount of revenue, although this is not what happens in practice (see Chapter 1).

A key aspect of wealth accumulation is that it operates in a self-reinforcing way; wealth begets wealth. High earners are able to save more (i.e. the marginal propensity to save increases with income), meaning that they are able to invest more and thereby ultimately accumulate more wealth. Moreover, returns tend to increase with wealth. Wealthy taxpayers, who tend to have more diversified asset holdings, are in a better position to invest in riskier assets which will tend to generate higher returns. The ability of the wealthiest taxpayers to generate higher average returns may also come from their access to wealth management and tax planning services as well as different investment opportunities (e.g. mutual funds that have entry requirements) (Fagereng et al., 2016). Rich taxpayers are also more likely to obtain loans, which will in turn allow them to invest more and accumulate more wealth. Finally, it may be argued (see below) that wealth begets more power, which may ultimately beget more wealth. Overall, this means that, in the absence of taxation, wealth inequality will tend to increase.

Capital income taxes alone will most likely not be enough to address wealth inequality. If a tax is only levied on the return to investment, the post-tax return will largely – at least for the wealthiest taxpayers – not be consumed, but be added to the principal and re-invested, thereby generating further (and likely higher) returns and allowing wealth to continue accumulating. For individuals at the top of the wealth distribution, even in the cases where a large portion of post-tax returns to investment are consumed, it will most likely be in the form of luxury purchases such as high-value immovable and movable property, which will also end up increasing their capital stocks. This suggests the need to complement capital income taxes with a form of wealth taxation in order to address wealth inequality and this report argues that there is a strong case for an accompanying inheritance tax (see below). Capital income taxes could also potentially be designed in ways that enhance their effectiveness in addressing wealth inequality but this would need to be explored in future work.

There is a clear case on distributional grounds for taxing wealth transfers at death. Although there is limited evidence on the relative importance of inherited wealth in total wealth and in the persistence of wealth inequality, there is a strong case for taxing wealth transfers to reduce intergenerational inequality and increase equality of opportunity by reducing and dispersing wealth holdings at death. A recent study in the United Kingdom (Hood and Joyce, 2017) shows that inheritances increase with income: lifetime inheritances are 4.4% of net lifetime income for the top quintile and 3.6% for the bottom quintile, compared with around 2% for the second and third lifetime income quintiles. In addition, they highlight that today's elderly have more wealth to bequeath than their predecessors, largely because of higher homeownership rates and rising house prices, which means that the wealth of younger generations is more likely to depend on who their parents are than in the past. On the other hand, Elinder et al. (2015) find that inheritances in Sweden reduce inequality. Wealthier heirs inherit larger amounts, but less affluent heirs receive substantially larger inheritances relative to their pre-inheritance wealth. However, they find that if the revenues raised from inheritance taxes are redistributed to the less wealthy, then the total effect of inheritance taxation makes the wealth distribution more equal. Even though it shows that inheritances reduce inequality, the latter study can be viewed as supporting the case for progressive inheritance taxes, which would involve taxing large inheritances but not taxing or taxing at very low rates small inheritances received by poor taxpayers, to ensure that the equalising effect of inheritances identified in the study is not offset by inheritance taxes.

Additionally, there are meritocratic arguments for taxing inherited wealth more than self-made wealth (Piketty et al., 2013). Inheritances constitute an unearned advantage for recipients (Iara, 2015). From an equal opportunity perspective, wealth transfers can be viewed as a source of additional opportunity that is not linked to the recipient's effort and that should therefore be taxed, regardless of whether the donor has already paid income tax or capital gains tax on the assets (Boadway et al., 2010). As with wealth taxes, it makes sense to have an exemption level that avoids taxing the majority of people who leave small inheritances. This reduces the number of people subject to tax without losing much of the potential revenue.

In practice, however, and as discussed in more detail later, there are many factors that reduce the positive effects of net wealth taxes on equity. The narrowness of the tax base limits the actual progressivity of net wealth taxes. Some of the assets which are widely held by the wealthiest are often exempt or preferentially taxed. Part of the limited effect of the wealth tax on redistribution also comes from tax avoidance and evasion opportunities, which allow the wealthiest taxpayers to minimise their wealth tax burden. Other design features, in particular tax caps (see Chapter 4), limit the progressive effect of wealth taxes. Finally, limited effects on redistribution come from the limited revenues raised through wealth taxes.

Wealth provides benefits above and beyond income

According to this argument, taxpayers with high wealth have greater resources to draw from and should be taxed at a higher rate than taxpayers with fewer assets even if they earn the same level of income. Simply put, there is a difference in ability to pay between a taxpayer who earns an annual income of EUR 20 000 from a EUR 200 000 investment, and a taxpayer who earns a salary of EUR 20 000 a year (Rudnick and Gordon, 1996).

Indeed, wealth confers advantages over and above the income derived from wealth. In addition to the income it generates, wealth may bestow social status, power, greater opportunities, satisfaction, or provide an insurance value against unexpected future needs, and it has been argued that such benefits should be taxed (Meade, 1978). Besides, wealth can provide income without having to sacrifice leisure (McDonnell, 2013). In some cases, assets do not generate income but still provide the benefits mentioned above. In that sense, a wealth tax can be seen as a complement to income tax, reflecting the additional advantages and capacity provided by wealth. Others have argued, however, that because the benefits of holding wealth are not measurable, it would be difficult for the tax system to take them into account, and that those types of benefits typically accrue to the very wealthy, so that a separate wealth tax would only be justified, if at all, on taxpayers at the very top of the wealth distribution (Boadway et al., 2010).

An alternative way of taking into account the benefits that wealth confers would be through the use of wealth-testing for broader tax and benefit purposes. Tax systems in OECD countries typically do not use information on household net wealth to determine taxpayers' income tax liability. Information about taxpayers' wealth could be used to strengthen the fairness of the income tax and the benefit system. Tax privileges for private pension savings, for instance, could be made dependent on the level of household wealth. In theory, capital income taxes could also be designed to increase with both income and wealth. These issues could be examined in future work.

Net wealth taxes could be an efficient substitute for capital income taxes by encouraging a more productive use of assets

In addition to arguments for having a wealth tax on top of capital income taxes, there is an argument for having a wealth tax as a substitute for capital income taxes, which could encourage taxpayers to use assets more productively. Given that a wealth tax is imposed on accumulated assets irrespective of the income they generate (see above), it may encourage taxpayers to use assets more productively. For instance, if a household owns land which is not being used and therefore does not generate income, no income tax will be payable on it. However, if a wealth tax is levied, the household will have an incentive to make a more productive use of their land or to sell it to someone who will (McDonnell, 2013). It has been argued by some that imposing a presumptive tax on capital income can be viewed as a tax on "potential income" (see Box 3.2). Guvenen et al. (2017) developed a theoretical model which suggests that replacing capital income taxes with a wealth tax shifts the tax burden onto unproductive entrepreneurs and that this reallocation increases aggregate productivity and output. Indeed, efficiency gains can occur because capital is reallocated to high-return individuals, and because the higher return of high-return individuals can motivate the accumulation of greater saving (Fagereng et al., 2016). The argument here is that wealth taxes do not discourage investment *per se* but discourage investments in low-yielding assets and reinforce the incentives to invest in higher-yielding assets because there is an additional cost to holding assets, which is not linked to the return they generate.

Box 3.1. A presumptive tax on capital income or a net wealth tax as a tax on 'potential income'?

According to Faulk, Martinez-Vazquez and Wallace (2006), presumptive income taxes do not necessarily have to be seen as an approximation of the tax liability under normal tax accounting rules but they could also be interpreted as a measure of the tax burden on "potential" income. The authors focus on the taxation of the return on human capital. Depending on the individual's work effort, potential income may be more or less than earned income. A tax on potential income rewards those individuals that work harder and earn more than their potential income and penalises those individuals that earn less than their potential income. However, this clearly does not imply that a potential tax would not create any economic distortion. Faulk, Martinez-Vazquez and Wallace (2006) explain that this type of tax may have an impact on human capital accumulation, for instance.

A certain element of "potential" taxation on capital income at the business level could be found in France (the 'forfait' system) and Israel (the 'tachisv' system). In France, for instance, unincorporated businesses could agree with the tax administration to be taxed for a number of years based on estimated income, following sophisticated and detailed administrative procedures, instead of on actual income (Wallace, 2002).

The Dutch presumptive capital income tax has sometimes been referred to as a tax on "potential" income (see for instance Stevens et al., 2006). It could be argued that the Dutch government holds the presumption that, over a longer time horizon, the potential return that could be earned if savings would be invested with due diligence is 4%. Individuals who own less wealth (not taking the owner-occupied house into account) may want to take less risk and will therefore earn a lower return on their savings. This implies that government should impute a "potential" return which increases with wealth. In 2017, this element was introduced (see Box 4.1).

However, there are limitations to this argument. There may be cases where asset returns do not reflect higher productivity and where recurrent net wealth taxes may therefore not support an efficient allocation of resources. Above-market returns may for instance be the result of luck or privileged market access (Kopczuk and Shrager, 2014). Favouring high returns may also discourage potentially highly profitable investments, such as investments in start-ups which are likely to generate low returns in their first few years of operation. In addition, even if there might be efficiency gains from replacing capital income taxes with wealth taxes, in practice, wealth taxes generally come on top, rather than as a replacement of, capital income taxes. Finally, from an equity point of view, as discussed earlier, favouring the holders of high-return assets implies imposing lower effective tax burdens on the wealthiest households.

Net wealth taxes could be a substitute for taxes on capital gains

A net wealth tax could also be a substitute for capital gains taxes. If capital gains are lightly taxed or not taxed at all, and if it is easy for taxpayers to avoid capital gains taxes by converting taxable personal capital income into untaxed or lightly taxed capital gains, then a net wealth tax can be seen as a substitute for capital gains taxation on the appreciation of assets.

As mentioned already, a key difference between a capital gains tax and a net wealth tax is that a wealth tax is theoretically levied on an accrual basis. Under the assumption that the wealth tax base is kept up to date through regular asset valuations, the appreciation in asset values is taxed every year under a wealth tax. In contrast, under income taxation, taxes are levied on a realisation basis, meaning that taxes are levied when assets are sold on the increase in value between the time they were purchased and sold. Accrual-based taxation has a number of advantages. First, it prevents the deferral of realised capital gains and lock-in effects, which ultimately result in an inefficient allocation of capital. Second, accrual-based taxation enhances fairness as appreciations in asset values are a better reflection of taxpayers' current wealth. However, taxation on an accrual basis involves numerous practical difficulties, and if asset values are not regularly updated, the wealth tax becomes more comparable to a tax on a realisation basis.

An alternative could be a wealth accretion tax. Instead of taxing total net wealth, governments could consider taxing only the changes in household wealth under a capital or wealth accretion tax on an accrual basis, or mark-to-market tax as the tax is also called. According to the Schanz-Haig-Simons income concept, the annual accretion of wealth, measured in real terms, is the most ideal income tax base (OECD, 2006; Cnossen and Bovenberg (2001)). Under mark-to-market accounting, all assets would be valued at their fair market value at the end of each fiscal year and the taxpayer would be taxed on this wealth increase upon accrual. Mark-to-market accounting is a significant departure from generally applied realisation accounting and would prevent timing distortions in that taxpayers would no longer have a tax-induced incentive to realise (tax-deductible) losses and to defer the realisation of taxable capital gains.

A mark-to-market tax would allow full loss offset in the fiscal year when the loss is incurred or would allow losses to be carried forward (Toder and Viard, 2016) and to be offset against future mark-to-market tax liability. Miller (2005) has suggested introducing a mark-to-market tax only for very high-income and high-wealth individuals, trusts and companies, where the threshold would be set such that only the very wealthy and highest income-earning individuals would be affected. Cnossen and Bovenberg (2001) have suggested introducing a mark-to-market tax to tax the returns on financial products but to tax the returns on real estate under a realisation-based capital gains tax, with interest on the deferred tax to reduce lock-in effects.

Another option would be to design the net wealth tax as a minimum tax which is creditable against any current or future capital income and/ or gains tax liability. As such, the wealth tax could be used to reduce the lock-in effects generated by a realisation-based capital gains tax. Alternatively, the wealth tax which would tax the normal return to investment could be combined with a capital gains tax levied only on the infra-marginal return on savings in order to prevent double taxation of the normal return on savings.

Net wealth taxes could be used as a substitute for inheritance taxes

By reducing the amount of net wealth that can be passed on to future generations, a net wealth tax has features that are common to inheritance taxes. Both taxes are levied on net wealth, but one is levied on a taxpayer's total net assets on a recurrent basis, while the other is only levied on wealth transfers at death. They nevertheless both reduce the amount of wealth that can be transferred by donors to recipients. Of course, to be equivalent to an inheritance tax, a recurrent net wealth tax would have to be levied at a very low rate. Indeed, even a low recurrent wealth tax liability results in a high effective tax rate when the total amount of net wealth taxes paid is expressed as a share of taxpayers' estates. If a household owns EUR 100 000 in net wealth over time, which is taxed at 0.5% under a recurrent net wealth tax, it will have to pay EUR 500 in wealth tax every year. If the same amount of net wealth is held for 40 years, the total amount of wealth taxes that will have been paid will amount to EUR 20 000 (for simplicity, the time value of money is ignored), which is equivalent to an inheritance tax of 20% on the EUR 100 000 transferred as a bequest (EUR 20 000/EUR 100 000 or 40 x 0.5%).

Nevertheless, a net wealth tax remains an imperfect substitute for inheritance taxes. A net wealth tax is levied on all accumulated wealth including the wealth that households use to finance consumption at a later stage in their life, in particular when they retire. The effective inheritance tax burden imposed by a yearly net wealth tax increases rapidly if part of the household's wealth is consumed during retirement. This is less true, however, if a net wealth tax is levied only on very wealthy taxpayers, whose wealth will largely be transferred to recipients as opposed to consumed during the donors' lifetime. It should be mentioned as well that if a country has a very high level of wealth inequality, reducing wealth gaps through income and wealth transfer taxes may take time and that, under such circumstances, there may be a role for a net wealth tax to address wealth inequality.

Promoting human capital investment

Human capital is always exempt under net wealth taxes. This results from a number of considerations, including the fact that human capital is very difficult to value, that it is not directly transferrable or convertible into cash, and that there is uncertainty about the durability of its value (McDonnell, 2013). Therefore, a wealth tax lowers the net return on real and financial assets relative to the returns on investments in human capital.

Thus, wealth taxes encourage investment in human capital, which may in turn have positive effects on growth. Human capital is a critical driver of long-run economic growth. This implies that a wealth tax may be less harmful to economic growth than commonly believed as it can encourage a substitution from physical to human capital formation (Heckman, 1976 in Hansson, 2002).

The case against net wealth taxes

This section assesses the arguments that have been made against net wealth taxes. This section starts by looking at the arguments against wealth taxes on efficiency grounds; it then looks at the equity-based arguments against net wealth taxes; and it concludes with the practical limitations of net wealth taxes. The practical limitations of net wealth taxes should be distinguished from the theoretical arguments against net wealth taxes, however, given that they may, at least to some extent, be addressed through good tax design and administrative improvements.

Double taxation

Double taxation is a popular objection to net wealth taxes, but it is far from unique to wealth taxes. One of the most common objections to individual net wealth taxes is that they are unfair because they generate double (or even triple) taxation. If wealth is accumulated from wage earnings, savings or personal business income, then these flows will have in many cases already been taxed. If households accumulate wealth in order to smooth consumption over their lifetime, their wealth will be taxed again when it is used for consumption. However, multiple levels of taxation are far from unique to wealth taxes. Consumption taxes, for instance, are paid out of post-tax income.

The validity of the double taxation argument also depends on countries' overall tax burden on capital and on the design of the wealth tax. For instance, if wealth primarily comes from asset revaluation, as Weale (2010) argues is the case in the United Kingdom, and if capital gains are not (or not adequately) taxed, then taxes on wealth do not constitute double taxation. The occurrence of double taxation also depends on how many taxpayers are subject to the net wealth tax. At lower wealth levels, as wealth is likely to be in large part accumulated for later consumption, wealth taxation indeed adds a third layer of taxation on a base that has been taxed as earned income and will be taxed as consumption. For very wealthy taxpayers, on the other hand, it is likely that part of their wealth comes from capital income, which is taxed at effective rates that vary widely and that can be low, and might not be used for later consumption, which means that double taxation is likely to be much more limited. Thus, a wealth tax that is only levied on the very wealthy might not generate much double taxation in practice. This underlines the importance of looking at wealth taxes as part of a broader tax system and of assessing how it interacts with other taxes (Brys et al., 2016).

In the case of inheritance taxes, it may be argued that the double taxation argument is weaker (Piketty et al., 2013). As with net wealth taxes, double taxation is a commonly stated objection to estate and inheritance taxes: people have already paid income tax or capital gains tax on their income before it was used to purchase assets which will be taxed again at death. However, in the case where the wealth transfer tax is levied on the recipient rather than on the donor (i.e. an inheritance tax rather than an estate tax), there is no double taxation of the donor himself and the inherited wealth is also only taxed once in the hands of the recipient. Moreover, as is the case with net wealth taxes, there might be instances where the inheritance tax will be the first time asset returns are taxed. For example, increases in the value of main residences are often exempt from capital gains tax. As a consequence, while the purchase price may well have been paid out of taxed earnings, any subsequent increases in value – which have been far greater than normal returns in recent years – will not have been subject to tax (Boadway et al., 2010).

Distortions to savings and investment

The main efficiency related argument against net wealth taxes is that – in a way that is comparable to capital income taxes – they distort saving behaviours. Standard economic models of optimal taxation assume that households save in order to consume tomorrow instead of today. Savings are therefore related to expenditure on future consumption. If the return on savings is taxed, the decision to postpone consumption and the intertemporal allocation of resources is distorted by the tax system, as the tax drives a wedge between the prices of consumption at different dates.

Two seminal models have concluded that the optimal capital income tax rate is zero. In their two-period model with one period of work, weak separability between consumption and leisure in each period, identical preferences across households and with the condition that non-linear taxes on labour earnings can be levied, Atkinson and Stiglitz (1976) show that there is no case for taxing future consumption and therefore the return to savings. The second major model concluding that capital should not be taxed was developed by Judd (1985) and Chamley (1986). They found that, in a dynamic Ramsey model, assuming infinitely-lived agents and no distortions in the economy, the long-run optimal tax on capital is zero.

However, these models rely on assumptions that are highly restrictive and that have to a large extent been empirically invalidated, with many new models concluding that positive capital taxes are optimal. Assumptions behind these models are highly stylised – including infinite time horizons, altruistic dynasties or the separability of preferences, for instance – and have often been questioned (e.g. Banks and Diamond, 2010). Many recent optimal tax theory models have refuted the optimality of zero capital taxation. For instance, Aiyagari (1995), by introducing non-trivial heterogeneity, assuming that markets are incomplete and allowing for uninsured idiosyncratic constraints, shows that there is a role for capital income taxation. Jacobs and Bovenberg (2010) show that it is optimal to tax capital income to reduce the distortions of the labour income tax on human capital investment. Straub and Werning (2014) also refute the optimality of a zero long-run tax on capital by revisiting and using the very logic of the models developed by Chamley and Judd.

As discussed above, wealth taxes do not operate exactly like capital income taxes and their effects on savings and investment will differ. While it may seem irrelevant for a taxpayer who has a total net wealth of EUR 10 million that earns a rate of return of 4% whether the government levies a tax of 30% on the capital income or a wealth tax of 1.2% on the capital stock – as both raise EUR 120 000 – there is an important distinction between the two. As discussed above, a tax on the stock of wealth is equivalent to taxing a presumptive return but exempting returns above that presumptive return. Where the presumptive return is set at the level of or at a level close to the normal - or risk-free – return to savings, a wealth tax is economically equivalent to a tax on the normal return to savings, which is considered to be inefficient. Indeed, the taxation of normal returns is likely to distort the timing of consumption and ultimately the decision to save, as the normal return is what compensates for delays in consumption (Mirrlees et al., 2011). As discussed below, it is also unfair that the wealth tax liability does not vary with returns, which implies that the effective wealth tax burden decreases when returns increase.

The potentially large distortive effect of wealth taxes on savings also comes from the fact that when wealth taxes are levied, they are often imposed *on top of* capital income taxes. If imposed on top of high income taxes, a net wealth tax can significantly increase marginal effective tax rates (METRs), in particular at higher inflation rates and lower real rates of return (see below), and in such circumstances not only discourage saving but potentially encourage dis-saving (i.e. consumption out of capital) (Messere et al., 2003). Evidence from a new OECD study (OECD, 2018) confirms that METRs can reach high levels in the presence of net wealth taxes (for details on the methodology, see Box 3.1). Figure 3.1 shows ETRs with and without net wealth taxes on different types of assets for taxpayers subject to the top PIT and net wealth tax rates in the countries that had net wealth taxes in 2017. The results show that net wealth taxes significantly raise the tax burden on capital income. In both France and Spain, METRs reached values above 100%, which means that the entire real return is taxed away and that by saving people actually reduce the real value of their wealth.

Box 3.2. Methodology for the calculation of METRs on savings

The marginal effective tax rates (METRs) presented in this report are extracted from a new OECD study (OECD, 2018) which estimates METRs across a range of savings vehicles for 38 OECD and key partner countries to assess the effect of tax systems on the incentives individuals face to save in different forms.

The METR methodology in this OECD study follows broadly the approach of the OECD's 1994 Taxation and Household Savings study (OECD, 1994), which itself drew on the methods used by King and Fullerton (1984). As emphasised in the OECD (1994) study, the appropriate way to analyse the effect of taxation on savings decisions is to examine the incentives faced by the taxpayer at the margin. The analysis therefore focuses on a saver who is contemplating investing an additional currency unit in one of a range of potential savings vehicles. The investment is a marginal investment, both in terms of being an incremental purchase of the asset, and in terms of generating a net return just sufficient to make the investment worthwhile (as compared to the next best savings opportunity).

The approach assumes a fixed pre-tax real rate of return and calculates the minimum post-tax real rate of return that will for that asset, at the margin, make the investment worthwhile. The METR can then be calculated as the difference between the pre- and post-tax rates of return (the savings income tax wedge) divided by the pre-tax rate of return. The calculations take into account different assumptions for the real rate of return, the inflation rate and the expected holding periods.

Source: OECD (2018)

Figure 3.1. Marginal effective tax rates (METRs) with and without wealth taxes on different assets

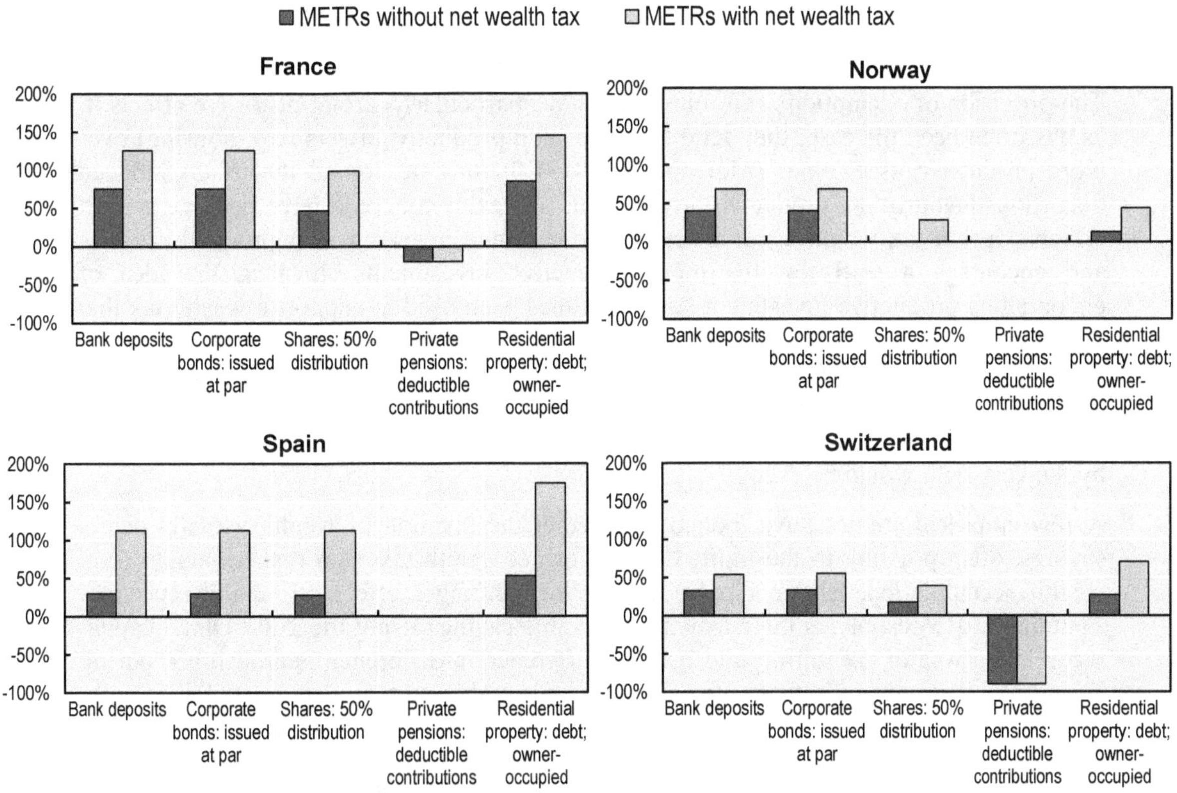

Note: The METR results are based on tax rules as of 1 July 2016.
Source: Data from OECD Taxation of Household Savings (OECD, 2018)

However, the cumulative nature of a net wealth tax and its potentially distortive effects depend on the rest of the tax system and interactions with other taxes on capital. Some of the countries that levy net wealth taxes do not impose taxes on the transfer of capital or on capital gains. For instance, in Switzerland, there is no capital gains tax; in Norway, the inheritance tax was repealed; and in the Dutch system, the tax on assumed income from savings and investments replaces the taxation of the actual income flows from these assets (Lawless and Lynch, 2016). In France[1] and Spain, on the other hand, in addition to net wealth taxes, the government levies taxes on capital transfers and taxes on capital gains. Figure 3.1 shows that, in contrast to Norway and Switzerland, the combination of personal capital income taxes and net wealth taxes results in very high METRs in France and Spain.

Beyond effects on the overall level of savings, net wealth taxes are also likely to affect the composition of savings. Adverse effects on savings and investment may also come from the distortions in the choice between different types of savings vehicles that wealth taxes generate through exemptions and reliefs. It can be assumed that if the tax base is narrow, there will be strong effects on the *composition* of savings, while if the tax base is broad, the wealth tax might have stronger effects on the *overall level* of savings. In practice, many categories of assets are exempt under net wealth taxes or benefit from reliefs or preferential valuation, which provides incentives to alter portfolio allocation away from that which would be optimal in a no-tax world (e.g. investing in assets with the lowest tax liability or those where valuation is most difficult). In practice, METR results reveal significant variations across asset types. Some assets tend to be particularly tax-favoured compared to others. Figure 3.1 shows in particular that pension savings are not taxed under net wealth taxes in any of the countries that currently have net wealth taxes.

The provision of exemptions and reliefs will have particularly strong distortive effects if, as has often been the case, they tend to favour non-productive assets (e.g. housing) over more productive asset types (McDonnell, 2013). It may be argued that if tax-induced distortions favour more productive investments, a wealth tax could have positive growth effects. Such a tax would lower incentives to continue investing in unproductive assets and encourage a shift towards more productive investments. In fact, the idea of encouraging productive investment has sometimes been used to support a wealth tax that would be levied exclusively on high value immovable property as opposed to overall net assets. Nevertheless, drawing a clear distinction between productive and unproductive assets is challenging. Besides, in the case of a wealth tax levied exclusively on high-value immovable property, equity might be reduced as financial capital, which is mostly owned by the very rich, would be exempt.

A few empirical studies have looked at whether the taxation of wealth actually deters savings, often pointing to the limited effects of net wealth taxes on real behaviour (e.g. wealth accumulation, labour supply) and to their stronger effect on wealth reporting. Zoutman (2015) estimates the elasticity of taxable savings using the 2001 Dutch capital income and wealth tax reform and using a difference-in-difference approach comparing households that are similar in terms of income and wealth but that were treated differently by the tax reform. He finds that an increase in the capital income and/or wealth tax leads to a relatively small loss in accumulated wealth: depending on the specification and the sample, a 1% increase in the current Dutch wealth tax of 1.2%, leads to a reduction in household savings between 0.10-0.17%. Using tax record data from Sweden, Seim (2017) estimates that net-of-tax-rate elasticities of taxable wealth were comprised between 0.09 and 0.27. His analysis also finds that these small but positive elasticities appear to reflect tax avoidance and evasion. Brülhart et al. (2017), on the other hand, find a stronger sensitivity of wealth holdings to wealth taxation in their analysis of wealth taxes in Switzerland. A 0.1 percentage-point increase in wealth taxes leads to 3.4% lower wealth holdings in their cross-canton data, substantially exceeding standard estimates of the elasticity of taxable income. However, their study also seems to suggest stronger effects on wealth reporting than on real behaviour with their results showing that taxpayers bunch below the tax threshold, that observed responses are driven by changes in wealth holdings rather than mobility, and that financial wealth is somehow more responsive than non-financial wealth.

Unfortunately, these studies cannot be used to draw conclusions on what the real effects of wealth taxes would be if tax avoidance and evasion opportunities were severely restricted. These studies generally suggest that real responses to wealth taxes are not significant in the presence of tax avoidance and evasion opportunities but the effects of wealth taxes on real behaviours would likely be much stronger if avoidance and evasion opportunities were severely restricted. These findings are consistent with the hierarchy of behavioural responses to taxation in Slemrod (1992), with decisions regarding the timing of transactions being the most responsive to tax changes, followed by avoidance, and real behaviours exhibiting the lowest degree of responsiveness. Taxpayers tend to respond in real terms (e.g. savings, labour) as a last resort, when avoidance and evasion opportunities are not available.

Regarding taxes on wealth transfers, their effects on savings will largely depend on bequest motives (e.g. accidental, strategic, altruistic or 'joy of giving'). For instance, unintentional transfers (e.g. when assets are accumulated or held for the owner's personal use for retirement or risk prevention) by definition have no impact on behaviour and can therefore be taxed more heavily without generating an efficiency loss. However, given that not all bequests are accidental and that they are often at least partly planned by donors, taxes on inherited wealth will always affect donors' saving and consumption decisions to some extent (Mirrlees et al., 2011). That being said, determining the intent of a donor is extremely difficult and there is usually more than one motive (Kopczuk, 2012), so for administrative reasons countries do not distinguish between bequest motives, leading to all wealth transfers being taxed together. In addition, inheritance taxes are expected to have an impact on recipients' saving and labour decisions: by reducing post-tax inheritances, they may give recipients stronger incentives to work and save themselves. Empirically, the evidence on the effects of wealth transfer taxes is mixed, but generally suggests a negative – but small – overall effect on donors' savings (Mirrlees et al., 2011).

Negative effects on entrepreneurship and risk-taking

Another efficiency related argument is that a net wealth tax reduces the amount of capital available, which may in turn affect entrepreneurship and business creation as access to capital is an important determinant of an individual's propensity to start a business (Hansson, 2010). Negative effects on entrepreneurship are even greater if business assets are (partly) taxed under the net wealth tax.

A key difference between income and wealth taxes is the treatment of losses, however, which has implications for risk-taking and entrepreneurship. Taxation is often believed to discourage risk-taking by capturing part of the return to risky investments. A competing view, however, is that, in cases of risk-averse investors and (perfect) loss offset, the taxation of income may in fact encourage risk-taking by absorbing a portion of the risk associated with risky investments (Domar and Musgrave, 1944). Under a net wealth tax, however, if income is zero or negative, the tax liability will still be positive if the capital value of the assets remains positive. In practice, new entrepreneurs which tend to generate low, or even negative, profits in their first few years of operation would still face a wealth tax liability. Thus, a heavy net wealth tax which is unlinked to income might discourage entrepreneurship relative to an income tax with (perfect) loss offset.

However, there are ways in which a wealth tax replacing an income tax may actually stimulate risk-taking and entrepreneurship. Taxpayers starting a business are likely to do so because in the longer run they expect to earn high returns compensating for the risks they have taken. As discussed, a tax on the stock of wealth is equivalent to taxing a presumptive return but exempting returns above that presumptive return, including returns to risk. In that sense, a wealth tax may stimulate entrepreneurship and risk-taking (in particular if the net wealth tax replaces taxes on capital income). Overall, it is therefore difficult to firmly argue that wealth taxes would have negative effects on entrepreneurship. The magnitude of the effects of wealth taxes on entrepreneurship is also unclear as business assets are often excluded from the wealth tax base in practice.

How assets are valued in the wealth tax base is also important when it comes to assessing how a wealth tax affects risk-taking. If assets are taxed on book values, the wealth tax liability will not vary with the business cycle and therefore the effective tax rate will be low in good times (i.e. low book/market value ratio) and high in bad times. On the contrary, if the wealth tax is based on market values and assuming that market values are regularly updated, then the effective tax rate will be constant over the business cycle. So a wealth tax based on market values (e.g. for listed firms) will be more neutral with respect to investors taking risks than a wealth tax based on book values (e.g. for non-listed firms) which increases the required return of risk-averse investors. On the other hand, book values may be significantly lower than market values (as is the case in Norway, for instance) and therefore a wealth tax may give an incentive to invest in non-listed firms relative to listed firms. This highlights the importance of setting the right tax base and the possible consequences of not doing so.

Inheritance taxes may also have a detrimental impact on entrepreneurship, particularly on family-owned businesses. Estate or inheritance taxes may discourage entrepreneurship by reducing the post-tax value of wealth transfers. Indeed, entrepreneurs might be less likely to start a business if they anticipate that a large portion of their business will be taxed when it is transferred to their heirs. High inheritance taxes may also make it difficult for family businesses to survive the death of their founders. To address these concerns, countries often provide inheritance tax relief for close-held/family businesses. However, the corollary of special tax treatments and reliefs is increased risks of tax planning and avoidance.

Liquidity concerns

Liquidity issues are a major equity concern regarding wealth taxes. The relationship between income and wealth is imperfect (see Chapter 2), which means that some households – the so-called "wealthy hand-to-mouth" (Kaplan et al., 2014) – have valuable assets which make them liable to the wealth tax but limited realised income with which to pay the tax. A substantial wealth tax bill combined with a low current income may result in assets needing to be sold in order to pay the tax, although the magnitude of the liquidity issue depends on how liquid assets are and on the level of the wealth tax. As will be discussed in greater detail in Chapter 4, liquidity issues can be mitigated through different measures, including by allowing tax liabilities to be spread over time or to be accumulated until assets are sold or inherited.

Liquidity issues also arise in the case of estate or inheritance taxes. A case where liquidity might be a real concern is for family-owned businesses where recipients are forced to sell parts or all of the business to pay the tax but, as mentioned above, many countries have special tax provisions lowering the tax liability in the case of family-business wealth transfers. However, liquidity constraints are less of a concern when inherited property has multiple recipients and has to be sold anyway to divide the value amongst the recipients (Boadway et al., 2010).

Penalisation of low-return and less diversified assets

From an equity perspective, a net wealth tax penalises the holders of low-return assets. As discussed already, because net wealth taxes do not tax the actual return earned on assets but are equivalent to the taxation of a presumptive return, the effective tax rate decreases when actual returns increase. Using the example of France in 2016, Figure 3.2 shows ETR results under different return scenarios and confirms that the wealth tax burden is heavier in a low-return setting. This may have negative equity effects. Indeed, there is evidence of heterogeneous returns that are positively correlated with wealth (Fagereng et al., 2016), which may be explained by the fact that wealthy investors tend to be less risk averse and allocate a much larger share of their financial portfolios to risky assets (Bach et al., 2015), have better access to financial expertise (economies of scale in wealth management) or might have better financial education and access to more lucrative investment opportunities. This means that if the wealth tax applies to (part of) the middle class, it might have regressive effects. For instance, taxpayers with a large portion of their assets in regular savings accounts, for which the rate of return is close to zero, are taxed for a return they generally did not realise, while wealthier taxpayers who have invested a lot of their savings in shares tend to accrue higher gains than they are taxed for. To avoid these negative equity effects, this would imply that a country that has a wealth tax should exempt some amount of bank deposits or have a high overall exemption threshold to ensure that only the wealthy are subject to the tax and/or levy the wealth tax at progressive rates.

Figure 3.2. METRs in France under different real return scenarios (2%, 3% and 4%) in 2016

METRs for taxpayers at 500% of the average wage and for top income and wealth taxpayers

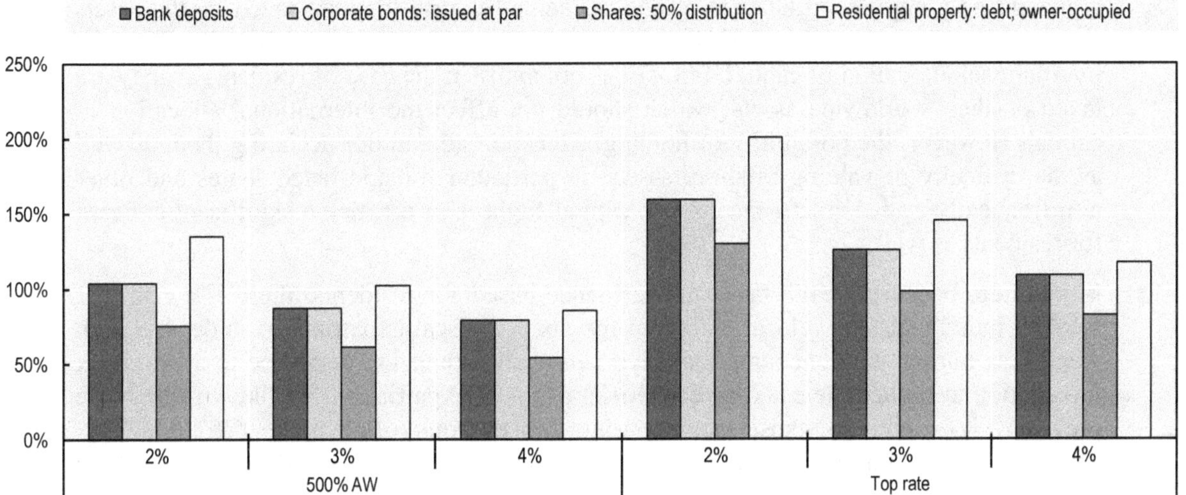

Note: The METR results are based on tax rules as of 1 July 2016.
Source: Data from OECD Taxation of Household Savings (OECD, 2018)

In addition, taxing a presumptive return below the actual return earned on savings provides greater tax savings to more wealthy households. Although wealth tax liabilities will increase with the amount of household wealth, the tax savings as a result of the taxation of a presumptive return below the actual return on savings will increase with the amount of wealth. One might therefore argue that, in this case, replacing personal capital income taxes with a net wealth tax will have regressive effects on the amount of tax savings as it provides higher tax savings to wealthier households. The opposite result holds if the presumptive return exceeds the actual return on savings.

Net wealth taxes may also be perceived as unfair given that the assets held predominantly by the wealthiest taxpayers often benefit from a more favourable tax treatment. Equity issues will arise with narrow tax bases, in particular if broadly-held assets are taxed but more mobile assets held primarily by the wealthiest taxpayers are exempt or taxed favourably. For instance, taxing favourably financial and business wealth – which is mostly held by households at the top of the income distribution (see discussion in Chapter 2) – while imposing a high tax burden on residential property may have detrimental equity effects as most of the middle class's wealth is tied up in immovable property. This is another strong argument for having a high exemption threshold to avoid possible negative equity effects.

Horizontal inequity over the lifecycle

A wealth tax might generate horizontal inequities over the lifecycle. If the net tax base is broad and low levels of wealth are taxed (i.e. the tax exemption threshold is low), households who save a lot when they are young to consume when they are older will pay more tax than households who spread their income more equally over their lifecycle. Chapter 2 shows a dynamic pattern in savings and wealth accumulation over the lifecycle and that on average households accumulate wealth throughout their working years, with wealth peaking in the years just prior to retirement, before declining.

Capital flight and fiscal expatriation

Capital flight has been a key argument against wealth taxes. In theory, the capital flight argument only applies in the case of non-residents because they are taxed on the assets they own within the taxing jurisdiction (source-based taxation) which will affect the international allocation of capital, but it does not apply in the case of residents as they are taxed on their worldwide assets, which should not affect the international allocation of capital. However, the possibility of holding assets abroad and not declaring them as well as the difficulty of valuing offshore assets, in particular for non-listed shares and other non-frequently traded assets, means that capital flight is in practice a significant concern for residents as well.

In addition, because wealth taxes are residence-based for residents, there is a risk that wealthy individuals can relocate to avoid the tax (i.e. fiscal expatriation). Indeed, a high wealth tax burden may encourage taxpayers to change their tax residence to a lower tax jurisdiction to reduce their tax burden. Risks of fiscal expatriation are likely to be more prevalent in countries whose neighbouring jurisdictions offer more favourable tax conditions. Regarding the potential effects of fiscal expatriation, on top of the immediate revenue losses, it might lead to a reduction in investment. However, whether fiscal expatriation has significant economic consequences on taxpayers' country of origin remains a question and will depend on whether fiscal expatriates maintain activities in their country of origin.

Empirical studies on the effects of wealth taxes on capital flight and fiscal expatriation are very limited. Pichet (2007) found evidence of significant capital flight out of France since the introduction of the net wealth tax. Zucman (2008), on the other hand, finds that wealth tax evasion in France is limited compared with the revenue generated by the tax. In the case of Switzerland, Brülhart et al. (2017) find evidence of low wealth tax-induced mobility. As mentioned above, tax-induced incentives for individuals to change their residency will depend on a variety of factors including the effective tax rate differentials with other countries or regions.

The evidence collected by governments on these issues tends to be anecdotal and difficult to interpret. In France, the Ministry of Finance has tracked the number of taxpayers subject to the wealth tax who leave and return to France. In 2014, 780 taxpayers subject to the net wealth tax left France, while 300 returns were registered. However, it is difficult to determine the extent to which decisions to move are motivated by tax factors or other personal or professional reasons. In the case of France, the significant increase in the number of net wealth taxpayers leaving France coincided with tax changes which generally lowered tax burdens on the very wealthy (decrease in top marginal PIT rates and introduction of the net wealth tax cap), which may suggest that taxpayers' departures were not primarily driven by tax considerations (*Conseil des prélevements obligatoires*, 2011). These studies also fail to capture the taxpayers who move abroad in anticipation of future wealth tax burdens, before they become liable to the wealth tax. Finally, as mentioned already, the economic repercussions of such fiscal exile are uncertain as taxpayers changing their residency for tax reasons can still continue to invest in their home country.

Taxpayers' locational decisions, in particular for the elderly, may also be affected by estate or inheritance taxes, although there is no clear empirical evidence of that. Bakija and Slemrod (2004) find that, in the United States, state estate taxes have a statistically significant negative effect on the number of federal estate tax returns filed in a state. This evidence seems consistent with the idea that some rich individuals flee states that tax them relatively heavily, although it may reflect other forms of tax avoidance as well. However, a number of other studies have found very limited effects of inheritance or estate taxes on migration patterns. For instance, Conway and Rork (2006), find no statistical evidence that bequest taxes affect inter-state migration patterns of elderly taxpayers in the United States. Looking at a much smaller country which is characterised by a greater degree of heterogeneity in sub-national bequest taxation, Brülhart et al., (2014) also find that cuts in bequest tax burdens across Swiss cantons have had little noticeable impact on the migration patterns of elderly taxpayers.

Tax avoidance and evasion

Increasing capital mobility has also enabled tax avoidance and evasion. The increasing mobility of financial assets as well as the use of tax havens, combined with the development of information and communication technology and the elimination of barriers to cross-border capital transfers (such as capital controls), have allowed taxpayers to move their capital offshore without declaring it and made the enforcement of capital income taxes and wealth taxes much more difficult (Krenek and Schratzenstaller, 2017). In fact, capital mobility has been a major factor behind the reduction of taxes on capital in the last few decades. The mobility of capital also has significant implications on the incidence of wealth taxes, as wealth taxes will likely end up bearing more heavily on less mobile forms of wealth, i.e. immovable property.

However, the recent progress made on international tax transparency and the exchange of information is increasing countries' capabilities to tax capital effectively. Information exchange agreements as well as further international cooperation on the exchange of information on request (EOIR), the automatic exchange of information (AEOI) and areas like beneficial ownership will reduce opportunities for tax evasion and ultimately allow countries to tax both capital and capital income more effectively. However, such efforts need to take into account that high-wealth individuals can change their tax residency and even their citizenship in response to high taxes, and that by limiting opportunities for tax avoidance and evasion, the real effects of taxes on capital – in particular on savings and investment – may be stronger (see above).

Domestic tax avoidance and evasion is also possible under a net wealth tax as there are a number of asset classes that are highly susceptible to non-disclosure or underreporting. As discussed below, some forms of wealth are difficult to value or can easily be hidden from tax authorities and the capacity of tax authorities to check non-disclosure and underreporting is often limited. Typical examples include household goods, vehicles, jewellery, artwork, etc. Relying on self-reporting also makes non-disclosure or underreporting more likely. This differs from withholding at source and third party reporting which are well-developed for many forms of capital income taxation such as dividends and interest; although in theory the same tools could be put in place for the taxation of capital stocks (Keen, 2014).

In addition, avoidance strategies are encouraged by the many exemptions and reliefs that are provided under net wealth taxes. As discussed in Chapter 4, there are different justifications for keeping certain assets out of the tax base or for taxing certain assets preferentially but tax exemptions and reliefs, in addition to narrowing the tax base, open up tax planning and avoidance opportunities. An important question, for instance, is whether the assets that taxpayers accumulate in their corporations should be taxed. This would be highly distortive but, if such assets are not taxed, wealthy taxpayers may avoid taxes by setting up corporations to accumulate their wealth tax-free. As mentioned already, from an equity perspective, tax planning opportunities through tax reliefs or exemptions are predominantly available to the wealthiest taxpayers who have diversified asset holdings and possibilities to restructure their assets and income.

Debt deductibility under net wealth taxes provides incentives to borrow and can encourage tax avoidance. While from an equity perspective it makes sense to tax net wealth, as net wealth is a better reflection of taxpayers' ability to pay, it implies that individuals will have an incentive to keep on borrowing funds for investment purposes as long as the return on the investment exceeds the interest that has to be paid. If the wealth tax base is narrow, taxpayers will have an incentive to avoid the tax by borrowing and investing in exempt assets or – if debt is only deductible when incurred to acquire taxable assets – taxpayers will have an incentive to invest part of their savings in tax-exempt assets and finance their savings in taxable assets through debt. In addition to opening up opportunities for tax avoidance, debt deductibility may raise financial stability concerns, by encouraging highly leveraged investments and the accumulation of high household debts, especially in economic downturns.

Empirical studies show clear evidence of wealth tax avoidance and evasion. As mentioned above, empirical studies on behavioural responses to wealth taxes tend to show that taxpayers respond more through tax avoidance and evasion than through changes in real behaviour. As mentioned already, in his analysis of the behavioural response to the wealth tax in Sweden, Seim (2017) estimates that the net-of-tax-rate elasticities of taxable wealth were between 0.09 and 0.27 and finds that these small but positive elasticities reflect tax evasion and avoidance rather than changes in savings. Using a panel of tax return micro-data from Catalan taxpayers for the 2011-14 period, Durán-Cabré et al. (2017) examine taxpayers' responses to the re-introduction of the Spanish net wealth tax in 2011. Their results provide empirical evidence that taxpayers facing higher tax rates reorganise the composition of their wealth in order to benefit from exemptions, also suggesting tax avoidance rather than real behaviour. More generally, Zucman (2015) finds evidence of a considerable and increasing amount of private wealth being hidden and managed in tax havens. His estimation is that around 8% of the global financial wealth of households is held in tax havens, three-quarters of which go unrecorded (Zucman, 2015).

Tax avoidance and evasion are also common with taxes on wealth transfers. As with net wealth taxes, tax avoidance is facilitated by the existence of estate or inheritance tax reliefs. Another tax avoidance strategy is the possibility to transfer wealth through lifetime gifts. That is why an inheritance tax needs to be complemented with a gift tax. A third major issue is related to trusts which, although they can be set up for perfectly legitimate reasons, can also potentially be used to avoid inheritance tax since they confer the benefits of wealth without transferring property ownership. Indeed, they are often used to separate the entitlement to the income that property generates from the entitlement to the property itself (Mirrlees et al., 2011). Thus, rules are also needed to prevent inheritance tax avoidance through the use of trusts. Addressing these issues is all the more critical as inheritance or estate taxes are levied at death and therefore leave significant time for tax planning.

Valuation and other administrative issues

In addition to the difficulties associated with tracing back wealth ownership, many forms of wealth are difficult to value. Valuation is difficult in the case of non- or infrequently traded assets (e.g. personal and household effects, pension rights, etc.). Partly as a consequence of valuation issues, many of these hard-to-value assets have been exempted from wealth taxes, eroding the tax base, distorting the choice of savings vehicles and creating opportunities for tax avoidance. Valuation issues are also significant in relation to non-listed firms and closely-held companies and are even greater for assets held overseas. Overall, it is much easier to determine the value of income flows than the value of capital stocks (Brown, 1991). As discussed in Chapter 4, however, there are some practical ways to address certain valuation issues – for instance, insured values can be used in the case of high-value jewellery or artwork, and exemptions can be granted for household effects under a certain threshold value (McDonnell, 2013).

Regularly updating asset values is an additional difficulty. Indeed, there is a trade-off between regularly updating asset values, which is costly both in terms of tax compliance and administration, and updating them less frequently, which may increase distortions and reduce fairness. There are, however, some ways to minimise the administrative and compliance burden associated with regularly updating asset values. For instance, asset valuations used for the residential property tax or the inheritance tax can be used for net wealth tax purposes as well. In addition, the value of taxpayers' total net wealth – or alternatively the value of particular asset classes – can be treated as fixed for a few years before being re-assessed (McDonnell, 2013).

The date of valuation can also raise issues. If assets are valued on 1 January, then the net wealth tax is partly levied on wealth that will be consumed later in the year. This distorts the timing of consumption decisions as taxpayers will have an incentive to bring their consumption forward to the end of the previous year. This argument is less convincing, however, if the net wealth tax base is broad. A lot of consumption occurring at the top of the wealth distribution is likely to consist in buying assets that would be taxed under a broad-based net wealth tax (e.g. cars, jewellery, artwork). On the other hand, if assets are valued at the end of the year, taxpayers may be taxed on wealth that they have accumulated during the year (i.e. savings) which implies that savings would be taxed twice in the same year.

In comparison, the taxation of wealth transfers at death tends to be less administratively costly. As opposed to net wealth taxes which require regularly updating asset values, valuing assets under an estate or inheritance tax, which involves determining their market value (or their realistic selling price) only occurs once, at the time of the transfer of assets between donors and recipients. Nevertheless, there are still some important valuation and administrative issues involved, including for instance complexities in relation to jointly held assets or due to the presence of two parties with different jurisdictional affiliations (Iara, 2015).

Summary and policy implications

This chapter has reviewed the arguments that have been made both for and against net wealth taxes. Those arguments are related to efficiency, equity and tax administration considerations. Many of the efficiency and equity effects of net wealth taxes are linked to the fact that they are levied regardless of actual returns and function like a tax on a presumptive (i.e. fixed) return. This chapter also discussed the effects of capital income taxes and taxes on wealth transfers to examine how these taxes interact with net wealth taxes and whether they can be complements to or substitutes for taxes on net wealth.

Overall, the chapter suggests that broad-based capital income taxation – including the taxation of capital gains – combined with well-designed inheritance taxes may be a more efficient and less administratively costly way of addressing wealth inequality. Overall, this chapter finds that, from both an efficiency and an equity perspective, there are limited arguments for having a net wealth tax on top of well-designed capital income taxes – including taxes on capital gains – and inheritance taxes, but that there are arguments for having a net wealth tax as an (imperfect) substitute for these taxes.

While there are important similarities between personal capital income taxes and net wealth taxes, the report shows that net wealth taxes tend to be more distortive and less equitable. As discussed in the chapter, a tax on the stock of wealth is equivalent to taxing a presumptive return to assets but exempting returns above that presumptive return. Where the presumptive return is set at the level of or at a level close to the normal - or risk-free – return to savings, a wealth tax is economically equivalent to a tax on the normal return to savings, which is considered to be inefficient. Indeed, the taxation of normal returns is likely to distort the timing of consumption and ultimately the decision to save, as the normal return is what compensates for delays in consumption (Mirrlees et al., 2011). This equivalence with a tax on a presumptive return also raises equity concerns as a wealth tax will favour the holders of high-return assets which tend to be wealthier taxpayers. There are also a number of practical difficulties associated with net wealth taxes, including valuation and liquidity issues. Finally, wealth taxes are generally imposed on top of capital income taxes, which can result in very high METRs on capital income. One of the areas where a wealth tax has advantages over capital income taxation, however, is that a net wealth tax is in theory levied on an accrual basis, which avoids the lock-in effects of taxation on a realisation basis, although this issue could possibly be addressed by taxing capital gains on accrual.

To strengthen progressivity, the way countries tax personal capital income could be revisited. In particular, progressive tax rates could be applied to personal capital income. As argued in previous OECD work (Brys et al., 2016), countries could consider introducing "dual progressive income tax" systems which would tax capital income under a separate rate schedule at progressive rates. The rate schedule could exempt or tax at low rates total household capital income below a minimum threshold. This could also encourage taxpayers at the bottom of the income and wealth distribution to save more, which could ultimately contribute to reducing wealth inequality. Finally, as mentioned above, consideration could be given to taxing capital gains upon accrual, noting the practical difficulties of doing so.

Inheritance taxes are also central to addressing the persistence of wealth gaps and tend to be less distortive than net wealth taxes. The report argues that capital income taxes alone will most likely not be enough to address wealth inequality and suggests the need to complement capital income taxes with a form of wealth taxation. The report finds that there is a strong case for an accompanying inheritance tax. The double taxation argument is weaker in the case of inheritance taxes than for net wealth taxes, as there is no double taxation of the donor and the inherited wealth is also only taxed once in the hands of the recipient. Effects on savings are also likely to be smaller than in the case of recurrent taxes on personal net wealth, and have generally been found empirically to be negative but small. Inheritance taxes are also easier to administer and comply with as they are only levied once. Finally, and perhaps more importantly, there are convincing meritocratic arguments for taxing inherited wealth more than self-made wealth. However, further work is needed to determine how to design inheritance taxes in a way that makes them both more efficient and fairer.

Overall, the report suggests that the merits of a net wealth tax cannot be assessed in isolation but depend on countries' overall tax systems and broader economic and social circumstances. Previous OECD work has already highlighted the need to look at tax systems as a whole and in the context of countries' economic and social circumstances (Brys et al., 2016). For instance, a net wealth tax may have more limited distortive effects and be more justified as a way to enhance progressivity in countries where the taxation of personal capital income is comparatively low. In practice, this implies that in countries with dual income tax systems that tax capital income at low and flat rates or in countries where capital gains are not taxed (e.g. Switzerland), there is a stronger justification for levying a net wealth tax. A similar argument can be made for countries that do not levy taxes on inheritances (e.g. Norway). Beyond tax considerations, there might also be greater justification for a wealth tax in a country exhibiting high levels of wealth inequality as a way to narrow wealth gaps at a faster pace.

Notes

[1] As mentioned previously, this chapter is based on the tax rules that were in place as of 1 September 2017. Since then, France has replaced its net wealth tax with a new real estate wealth tax, with effect from 1 January 2018.

References

Alvaredo, F. and E. Saez (2009): "Income and Wealth Concentration in Spain from a Historical and Fiscal Perspective", Journal of the European Economic Association, Vol. 7, No. 5, pp. 1140-67.

Aiyagari, S. R. (1995), "Optimal Capital Income Taxation with Incomplete Markets, Borrowing Constraints, and Constant Discounting", Journal of Political Economy, Vol. 103, No. 6, pp. 1158–75.

Bach, L., Calvet L. E. and P. Sodini (2017), "Rich pickings? Risk, return, and skill in the portfolios of the wealthy", CEPR Discussion Paper, No. 11734.

Bakija, J. and J. Slemrod (2004), "Do the rich flee from high state taxes? Evidence from Federal Estate Tax Returns", NBER Working Paper, No. 10645.

Banks, J. and P. A. Diamond (2010), "The Base for Direct Taxation" in The Mirrlees Review. Dimensions of Tax Design, edited by James A. Mirrlees et al., Oxford University Press, 548–648.

Bastani, S. and D. Waldenström (forthcoming), "What drives preferences for wealth redistribution? Evidence from linked survey and register data", preliminary version.

Boadway, R., Chamberlain E. and C. Emmerson (2010): "Taxation of Wealth and Wealth Transfers", in J. A. Mirrlees, S. Adam, T. Besley, R. Blundell, S. Bond, R. Chote, M. Gammie, P. Johnson, G. Myles and J. Poterba, eds., Dimensions of Tax Design: the Mirrlees Review, 8:737-836, Oxford University Press.

Brown, R. D. (1991), "A Primer on the Implementation of Wealth Taxes", *Canadian Public Policy / Analyse de Politiques*, Vol. 17, No. 3, pp. 335-350.

Brülhart, M., Gruber, J., Krapf, M. and K. Schmidheiny (2017), "Taxing Wealth: Evidence from Switzerland", *NBER Working Paper Series*, No. 22376.

Brys, B., Perret S., Thomas, A. and P. O'Reilly (2016), "Tax Design for Inclusive Economic Growth", *OECD Taxation Working Papers*, No. 26, OECD Publishing, Paris.

Chamley, C. (1986), "Optimal Taxation of Capital Income in General Equilibrium with Infinite Lives", *Econometrica,* Vol. 54, No. 3, pp. 607–622.

Cnossen, S. and L. Bovenberg (2001), "Fundamental tax reform in the Netherlands", *International Tax and Public Finance*, No.7, pp. 471-484.

Conseil des prélèvements obligatoires (2011), "Prélèvements obligatoires sur les ménages : progressivité et effects redistributifs", http://www.ladocumentationfrancaise.fr/rapports-publics/114000255/index.shtml

Conway, K. S. and J. C. Rork (2006), "State "death" taxes and elderly migration: the chicken or the egg?", *National Tax Journal*, Vol. 59, No. 1, pp. 97–128.

Domar, E.D., and R.A. Musgrave (1944), "Proportional income taxation and risk-taking", *Quarterly Journal of Economics*, Vol. 58, pp. 388-422

Durán-Cabré, J.M., Esteller-Moré, A. and M. Mas-Montserrat (2017), "Behavioural Responses to the (Re)Introduction of Wealth Taxes: Evidence from Spain", preliminary version.

Elinder, M., Erixson, O. and D. Waldenström (2015), "Inheritance and wealth inequality Evidence from population registers", Uppsala Center for Fiscal Studies Department of Economics Working Paper No. 2015:3.

Fagereng, A., Guiso, L., Malacrino, D. and L. Pistaferri (2016), "Heterogeneity and Persistence in Returns to Wealth", *NBER Working Paper Series*, No. 22822.

Faulk, D., Martinez-Vazquez, J. and S. Wallace (2006), "Taxing potential income: a second look at presumptive taxes", Georgia State University, Andrew Young School of Policy Studies, paper presented at the Annual Conference on Public Finance Issues.

Guvenen F., Kambourov, G., Kuruscu, B., Ocampo-Diaz, S., and D., Chenk, "Use It or Lose It: Efficiency Gains from Wealth Taxation", preliminary version.

Hood, A. and R. Joyce (2017), "Inheritances and Inequality across and within Generations", IFS Briefing Note BN192, The Institute for Fiscal Studies, London.

Iara, A. (2015), "Wealth Distribution and Taxation in EU Members", *Taxation Papers,* Working Paper No. 60, Brussels.

Jacobs, B. and L. Bovenberg (2010), "Human Capital and Optimal Positive Taxation of Capital Income", *International Tax and Public Finance* Vol. 17, No. 5, pp. 451-478.

Judd, K. L. (1985), "Redistributive Taxation in a Simple Perfect Foresight Model", *Journal of Public Economics*, Vol. 28, No. 1, pp. 59–83.

Hansson, A. (2010), "Is the Wealth Tax Harmful to Economic Growth?", *World Tax Journal*, 2010, Vol.10, No.1.

IMF (2014), "Fiscal Policy and Income Inequality", *IMF Policy Paper*, Washington, D.C.

Kaplan, G., Violante, G. L. and J. Weidner (2014), "The Wealthy Hand-to-Mouth", *Brookings Papers on Economic Activity*, Vol. 2014, No. 1, pp. 77-138.

Keen, M. (2014), "Taxing Wealth: Policy Challenges and Recent Debates", presentation for the ECFIN Taxation Workshop - Taxing Wealth: Past, Present, Future, 13 November 2014.

Kopczuk, W. (2012), "Taxation of Intergenerational Transfers and Wealth", *NBER Working Paper Series*, No. 18584.

Kopczuk, W. and A. Schrager (2014), "The Inequality Illusion: Why a Wealth Tax Won't Work", Snapshot, Foreign Affairs, https://www.foreignaffairs.com/articles/united-states/2014-05-15/inequality-illusion

Krenek, A. and M. Schratzenstaller (2017), "Sustainability-oriented Future EU Funding: A European Net Wealth Tax", *FairTax WP-Series* No.10.

Lawless, M. and D. Lynch (2016), "Scenarios and Distributional Implications of a Household Wealth Tax in Ireland", *ESRI Working Paper*, No.549.

McDonnell, T.A. (2013), "Wealth Tax: Options for its Implementation in the Republic of Ireland", *NERI Working Paper Series*, WP 2013/6.

Messere, K., De Kam, F. and C. Heady (2003), *Tax Policy: Theory and Practice in OECD Countries*, Oxford University Press.

Miller, D. S. (2005), "A progressive system of mark-to-market taxation", Tax Notes, November 21.Mirrlees, J., S. Adam, T. Besley, R. Blundell, S. Bond, R. Chote, M. Gammie, P. Johnson, G. Myles and J. Poterba (2011), *Tax by Design: The Mirrlees Review*, Oxford University Press for Institute for Fiscal Studies, Oxford.

Norwegian Ministry of Finance (2017), "The Norwegian Tax System - Main Features and Developments", Chapter 2 of the Budget Proposal on Taxes 2017: https://www.statsbudsjettet.no/upload/Statsbudsjett_2017/dokumenter/pdf/main_features_tax_system.pdf

OECD (2017), *Revenue Statistics: 1965-2016*, OECD Publishing, Paris. http://dx.doi.org/10.1787/9789264283183-en

OECD (2018), *Taxation of Household Savings*, Tax Policy Studies, OECD Publishing, Paris.

OECD (2007), *Fundamental Reform of Corporate Income Tax*, OECD Tax Policy Studies, No. 16, Paris, OECD Publishing. http://dx.doi.org/10.1787/9789264038127-en

OECD (2006), Fundamental Reform of Personal Income Tax, OECD Tax Policy Studies, No. 13, OECD Publishing. http://dx.doi.org/10.1787/9789264025783-en

Pichet, E. (2007), "The Economic Consequences of the French Wealth Tax", La Revue de Droit Fiscal, Vol. 14, pp. 1–25.

Piketty, T., Saez, E. and G. Zucman (2013), "Rethinking Capital and Wealth Taxation", preliminary version.

Rudnick, R. S. and R. K. Gordon (1996), "Taxation of Wealth", in V. Thuronyi (ed.), *Tax Law Design and Drafting*, International Monetary Fund.

Saez, E. and G. Zucman (2016), "Wealth Inequality in the United States since 1913: Evidence from Capitalized Income Tax Data", *Quarterly Journal of Economics*, Vol. 131, No. 2.

Schnellenbach, J. (2012), "The Economics of Taxing Net Wealth: A Survey of the Issues", Freiburger Diskussionspapiere zur Ordnungsokonomik, No. 12/5.

Seim, D. (2017), "Behavioral Responses to Wealth Taxes: Evidence from Sweden", *American Economic Journal* (forthcoming).

Silfverberg, C. (2002), "The Swedish Net Wealth Tax: Main Features and Problems", Stockholm Institute for Scandinavian Law.

Slemrod, J. (1992), "Do Taxes Matter? Lessons from the 1980s", *American Economic Review*, Vol. 82, No. 2, pp. 250–256.

Stevens, L.G.M., Albregtse, D.A. , Kavelaars, P., Smeets M.H.M. and Y.M. Tigelaar-Klootwijk (2006), "*Fiscaal Commentaar*," Inkomstenbelasting, 2006, Kluwer, Deventer.

Straub, L. and I. Werning (2014), "Positive Long Run Capital Taxation: Chamley-Judd Revisited", *NBER Working Paper Series*, No. 20441.

Toder, E. and A. D. Viard (2016), "A proposal to reform the taxation of corporate income", Tax Policy Center, Urban Institute & Brookings Institution, Washington D.C.

Weale, M. (2010), "Taxation of Wealth and Wealth Transfers: Commentary by Martin Weale" in *Dimensions of Tax Design: The Mirrlees Review*, Oxford University Press for the Institute for Fiscal Studies, Oxford University Press.

Zoutman, F. T. (2015), "The Elasticity of Taxable Savings", CESifo, 9th Norwegian-German Seminar on Public Economics.

Zucman. G. (2015), *The Hidden Wealth of Nations: The Scourge of Tax Havens,* University of Chicago Press.

Chapter 4. Net wealth tax design issues

This chapter examines practical tax design issues in countries that currently tax or have previously taxed individual net wealth. It largely draws upon countries' responses to the OECD Net Wealth Tax Questionnaire. This chapter highlights the differences in the ways that countries have implemented net wealth taxes in practice and identifies a number of good policy practices in the design of net wealth taxes.

This chapter is based on the tax rules that were in place as of 1 September 2017. Since then, France has replaced its net wealth tax ("*impôt de solidarité sur la fortune*") with a new real estate wealth tax ("*impôt sur la fortune immobilière*"), with effect from 1 January 2018.

This chapter provides an overview of net wealth tax design in countries that have or have had individual net wealth taxes. It draws upon countries' responses to the "OECD Net Wealth Tax Questionnaire" (see Annex A) and shows that countries that currently tax or have previously taxed net wealth have done so differently, with notable variations in tax design. Table 4.1 lists the countries that have responded to the questionnaire and whose net wealth taxes are discussed in this chapter. In addition to the four OECD countries that had individual net wealth taxes in 2017 (France, Norway, Spain and Switzerland), the chapter covers the net wealth taxes that were levied in Austria, Denmark, Germany, Ireland, Luxembourg, the Netherlands and Sweden. It should be mentioned as well that, in 2001, the Netherlands introduced a presumptive capital income tax that functions in practice like a net wealth tax (see Box 4.1). This chapter examines the different dimensions of net wealth tax design and compares how net wealth taxes have been designed and implemented across countries.

Table 4.1. Personal net wealth taxes covered in the chapter

	Countries	Name of the tax	Period of enforcement
Net wealth taxes in place in 2017	France[1]	*Impôt sur les grandes fortunes*, then renamed *Impôt de Solidarité sur la Fortune*	1982- Abolished in 1986 but re-introduced in 1989
	Norway	*Formuesskatt*	Introduced as a national tax in 1892
	Spain	*Impuesto sobre el Patrimonio*	1977 – 100% tax reduction introduced in 2008 but tax reinstated in 2011
	Switzerland	*Vermögenssteuer*	Gradual introduction by all cantons between 1840 and 1970
Historical net wealth taxes	Austria	*Vermögensteuer*	1954 - 1994
	Denmark	*Formueskat*	1903 - 1997
	Finland	*Varallisuusvero*	1919 - 2006
	Germany	*Vermögensteuergesetz*	1952 - 1997
	Ireland	Wealth Tax	1975 - 1978
	Luxembourg	Impôt sur la fortune (Net wealth tax)	1934 - 2006
	Netherlands	Vermogensbelasting	1965 - 2001
	Sweden	Förmögenhetsskatt (Wealth Tax)	1947, changed significantly in 1991, repealed in 2007

1. Chapter and table based on tax rules as of 1 September 2017. The French wealth tax has been replaced with a new real estate wealth tax since then.
Source: OECD Questionnaire on Current and Historical Net Wealth Taxes

Box 4.1. The capital income tax system in the Netherlands

The tax authorities in the Netherlands introduced the new Income Tax Act 2001 effective on January 1, 2001. The comprehensive personal income tax system that taxed both labour and capital income jointly at highly progressive rates was replaced with a schedular PIT system that taxed different types of income separately at different rates. The most significant component of the 2001 income tax reform was the introduction of the presumptive capital income tax (*vermogensrendementheffing*). In the Netherlands, the actual return on personally held wealth, in the form of dividends, interest or rental payments, is no longer taxed. Instead, a presumptive capital income tax on the value of the assets net of liabilities was introduced. The tax code assumes that all personally held assets – such as deposits, stocks, bonds and real estate (except owner-occupied property) – earn a presumptive rate of return, which is taxed at a proportional tax rate of 30%.

From 2001 until 2016, the presumptive rate of return was a uniform presumptive return of 4%. In 2017 some important new elements were introduced. First, a distinction was made between a presumptive rate of return on savings and a presumptive rate of return of investment (all other assets). Second, the introduction of three tax brackets with each bracket a presumptive mix of savings and other investment. The mix is based on the macro average portfolio mix per bracket. Third, the presumptive rates of return are yearly updated taking into account the actual return in the most recent year.

In the system that has been in force since 2017, the presumptive rate of return on savings in 2017 is following actual rates of return on savings by calculating a moving average over the last five years (1.63% for 2017). For investments, it is based on a long-term average annual return (5.50%). Each year the presumptive rate of return for investments is updated by 1/15th of the actual rate of return of the most recent year. Different portfolio allocations are then applied to different tax brackets, which result in progressive deemed returns.

Long-term average annual return on investments

	Return	Weight
Shares	8.25%	28%
Bonds	4.00%	12%
Real estate	4.25%	45%
Other assets	5.50%	15%
Average return	5.50%	100%

Deemed annual returns on savings and investments

	Deemed annual return
Savings	1.63%
Investments	5.50%

Deemed portfolio allocation and deemed return for the different tax brackets

Tax brackets	Deemed portfolio allocation		Deemed return
	Savings	Investments	
EUR 0 - EUR 25 000	Exempt		
EUR 25 000 - EUR 100 000	67%	33%	2.90%
EUR 100 000 - EUR 1 000 000	21%	79%	4.70%
Above EUR 1 000 000	0%	100%	5.50%

Although the presumptive capital income tax is an income tax (Stevens et al, 2006), it was equivalent to a net wealth tax of 1.2% between 2001 and 2016. Since 2017, deemed income increases with net wealth.

Government level

Net wealth taxes can be national level taxes, sub-central level taxes or a combination of both. In France, the wealth tax is a national level tax (replaced with a tax on real estate wealth as of 1 January 2018[1]). In Switzerland, wealth taxes are cantonal and municipal. Municipalities in most cantons apply the canton-level tax schedule but are free to choose the level of taxation by adding their own "multipliers" to the canton-level taxes (Brülhart et al, 2017). In Spain, the main structure of the wealth tax is regulated by the central government, but since the mid-1980s, along with the transfer of wealth tax revenues and the responsibility to administer net wealth taxes, regional governments have also been given limited legislative power to regulate the minimum threshold, tax rates and tax credits (Durán-Cabré et al. 2017). In Norway, the net wealth tax is split into a national and a local component. Among the countries that have historically had net wealth taxes, they were mostly national level taxes (Austria, Denmark, Finland, Ireland, Luxembourg, the Netherlands and Sweden), with the exception of Germany where the net wealth tax was levied by the federal states (Länder).

Tax unit

The practice has generally been to use the family as the tax unit in countries that currently have or previously had net wealth taxes. Family-based taxation implies that spouses and dependents are assessed and taxed jointly. Generally, the tax exemption threshold doubles for married couples but that is not always the case. In France, for instance, the tax exemption threshold and the tax schedule do not vary between single and married taxpayers, which implies that aggregating wealth increases the household's tax liability. Exceptions to family-based wealth taxes include Finland and Spain where the wealth tax was/is levied on an individual basis.

There are strong arguments for using the family as the tax unit. If spouses were to be taxed separately, it would be difficult to determine and split the ownership of household assets and to allocate the wealth of dependents to either one of the parents. In addition, in the case of a wealth tax with progressive rates and exemptions and deductions, taxing spouses separately would require closely monitoring transfers of assets between spouses. These issues do not arise if spouses are taxed jointly. In addition, it seems appropriate to aggregate dependents' wealth – very often derived directly from parents – with that of their parents, as parents generally exert control over that wealth (Brown, 1991). Finally, the disadvantages of family-based taxation under the income tax in terms of reduced incentives for second earners to participate in the labour market and work long hours are less of a concern under a wealth tax.

However, family-based taxation is not without problems. Joint taxation is usually only an option for married couples and not for other types of family structures (e.g. unmarried cohabitants) – a difference which is difficult to justify from the perspective of horizontal equity (but which might be explained by privacy arguments, as it is not the task of tax authorities to check if people live together or not). Moreover, it is not because couples are married that they actually share the ownership of their wealth. Finally, family-based wealth taxation may pose problems for countries that have elected individual-based income taxation.

The decision to double the tax exemption threshold for married couples or not involves a trade-off. If single wealth owners and married couples benefit from the same tax exemption threshold, couples may face a wealth tax-induced disincentive to get married. Alternatively, doubling the wealth tax exemption threshold gives a marriage bonus to households where both partners have very different levels of wealth.

Tax exemption thresholds

Net wealth taxes always exempt taxpayers under a certain level of net wealth to enhance equity. Figure 4.1, which models in a very simple way how the average effective wealth tax rate (i.e. wealth tax liability/net wealth) of a 1% net wealth tax evolves with net wealth, shows that an exemption threshold – and the level of that exemption threshold – has a strong effect on the progressivity of a wealth tax. By introducing an exemption threshold, the average effective wealth tax becomes a concave function. In fact, even with a flat tax rate, an exemption threshold can generate a lot of progressivity. A high exemption threshold also has the effect of lowering the average effective tax rates on the very wealthy.

Figure 4.1. Average effective wealth tax rate of a 1% net wealth tax

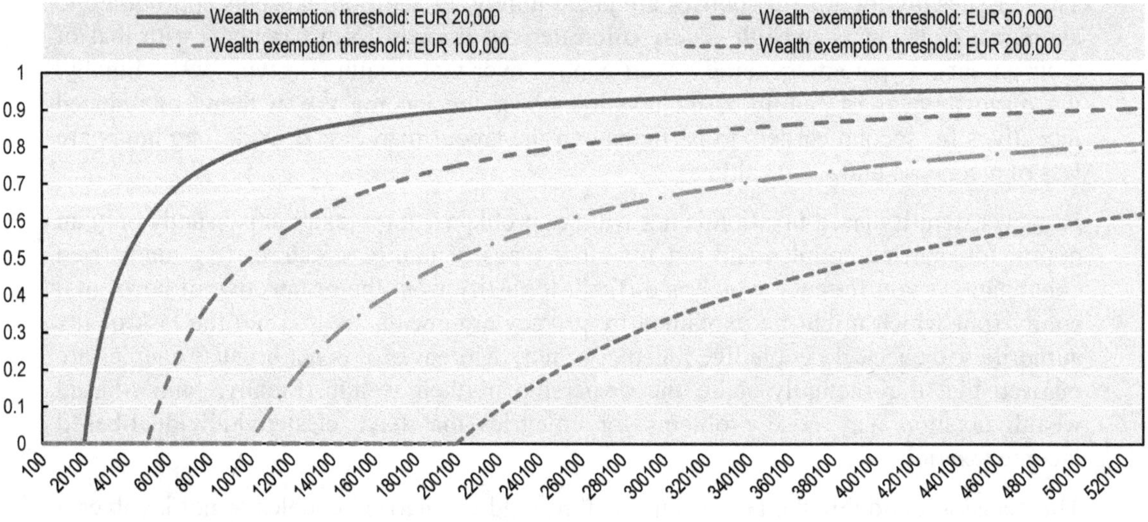

Source: Authors' calculations

Tax exemption thresholds have varied quite significantly across countries (Table 4.2). In some countries, the wealth tax only applies to the very wealthy, as is the case in France and Spain. In 2017, France had the highest exemption threshold, only taxing individuals and households with net wealth equal to or above EUR 1 300 000. In other countries, the wealth tax applies to a broader range of taxpayers. In Switzerland, for instance, despite variations across cantons, tax exemption thresholds are comparatively low: in 2014, they ranged from CHF 25 000 (USD 27 500) in the canton of Obwalden to CHF 200 000 (USD 220 000) in the canton of Ticino (Brülhart et al., 2017). Thus, net wealth taxes do not apply only to the wealthiest households but also affect a large portion of the middle class. Brülhart et al. (2017) report for instance that in the canton of Bern, 30% of all taxpayers and 41% of married households had a non-zero wealth tax liability over the 2001-2011 period. One of the explanations for these low tax exemption thresholds may be that Switzerland does not levy capital gains taxes and levies very limited recurrent taxes on immovable property (some cantons have them, others do not), and that net wealth taxes may partly replace these taxes.

Table 4.2. Net wealth tax exemptions thresholds in 2017 or in the latest year of operation, expressed in EUR

	Countries	Single taxpayer	Married couple
Net wealth taxes in place in 2017	France	1 300 000	1 300 000
	Norway	157 833	315 666
	Spain	700 000	1 400 000[2]
	Switzerland[2]	67 550	135 100
Historical net wealth taxes	Austria (1994)	No threshold[3]	No threshold[4]
	Finland (2006)	250 000	500 000[1]
	Germany (1997)	61 355	x
	Iceland (2015)	473 248	630 997
	Ireland (1978)	88 882	126 974
	Luxembourg (2006)	No threshold[4]	No threshold[4]
	Netherlands (2001)	90 756	113 445
	Sweden (2007)	166 214	221 619

Notes: For countries that abolished their wealth taxes before the introduction of the Euro, currency conversion rates on 1 January 2002 were used; for the other countries, currency conversion rates in the last year of operation of the wealth tax were used.

1. For Spain, each taxpayer is entitled to the EUR 700 000 allowance; in Finland, each taxpayer is taxed separately and entitled to the EUR 250 000 allowance.
2. Tax exemption thresholds in the Canton of Zurich used for Switzerland.
3. There was no specific threshold in Austria, but implicitly due to tax allowances persons with wealth below EUR 11 000 were exempt.
4. There was no absolute exemption threshold (in EUR) in Luxembourg but a relative threshold whereby only 50% of the "unitary value" of assets was taken into account for wealth tax purposes.

Source: OECD Questionnaire on Current and Historical Net Wealth Taxes

In recent years, tax exemption thresholds have generally been raised. The Norwegian tax exemption thresholds were NOK 750 000 for single taxpayers and NOK 1 500 000 for married couples in 2012. Since then, they have been increased progressively, respectively reaching NOK 1.48 million and NOK 2.96 million in 2017. In Spain, exemption thresholds were significantly raised when the net wealth tax was reintroduced in 2011. Prior to 2008, general exemption thresholds ranged from EUR 108 182 to EUR 150 000 depending on the region, while the central government threshold is now set at EUR 700 000. The exemption for the main residence was also almost doubled (Durán-Cabré et al., 2017). In France, the tax exemption threshold was raised in 2012 from EUR 800 000 to EUR 1 300 000. Increases in tax exemption thresholds were often motivated by the desire to avoid burdening the middle or upper-middle class, in particular as asset values – most notably housing prices – have increased. Such changes have significant effects on the incidence and equity effects of net wealth taxes.

Due in large part to differences in exemption thresholds, the share of taxpayers subject to the wealth tax has also varied quite substantially across countries. In France, only 351 152 tax households ("*foyers fiscaux*"), or slightly less than 1% of the total number of tax households, were subject to the net wealth tax in 2016. In Spain, there was a considerable decrease in the number of taxpayers subject to the wealth tax between 2007 and 2015, from 981 498 to 188 680, reflecting the significant increase in tax exemption thresholds (see above). In Norway, the share of taxpayers subject to the net wealth tax has been higher, estimated at about 11% of taxpayers in 2016. This share seems low given Norway's comparatively low exemption threshold but may partly be the result of the very favourable valuation rules for primary residences (see below). It should be mentioned as well that while the proportion of people paying net wealth tax in Norway has been reduced due to increases in the minimum allowance, the average amount of tax on the part of those who pay net wealth tax has increased in recent years (Norwegian Ministry of Finance, 2017). The highest number and share of total taxpayers subject to net wealth taxes by far is found in Switzerland, where a total of 5 150 529 taxpayers[2] were liable to net wealth taxes in 2016. Differences in numbers of taxpayers are to a large extent a consequence of variations in the levels of tax exemption thresholds, but also reflect the distribution of wealth in countries.

Differences in the levels of the exemption thresholds may in some cases – but not always – reflect differences in the range of taxed assets and in tax rates. For instance, in countries where tax rates are relatively high (e.g. Spain, France), exemption thresholds tend to be high as well. As shown in Figure 4.1, a high threshold implies that wealth above the threshold is taxed effectively at low average rates. High thresholds will therefore often be accompanied by high rates, otherwise tax revenues and ETRs will be low. However, this is not the case everywhere. For instance, the Norwegian wealth tax combines a low threshold and a relatively high tax rate, which makes it unusual and entails a much higher tax burden on the moderately wealthy compared to net wealth taxes in other countries (McDonnell, 2013; Schnellenbach, 2012).

In the discussion in Chapter 3, several arguments have been put forward to justify a high tax exemption threshold. The main justification for having a high exemption threshold is to support equity. Indeed, a high exemption threshold ensures that only the very wealthy pay the tax, prevents the taxation of lifecycle savings, and mitigates the issues related to taxing a presumptive return on assets (see Chapter 3), which end up penalising the holders of low-return assets. A high tax exemption threshold also has the benefit of limiting administrative and compliance costs. From a revenue raising perspective, since wealth is highly concentrated at the top of the wealth distribution, a net wealth tax should allow governments to raise significant revenues even if the exemption threshold is set at a high level (provided that the tax base is broad as recommended below). Ideally, the exemption threshold should also be revised annually or every few years to account for inflation.

Taxed assets, exemptions and reliefs

Under a net wealth tax, residents are typically taxed on their worldwide net assets, while non-residents are generally only taxed on their assets that are located within the taxing jurisdiction. Thus, net wealth taxes are a mix of source-based and residence-based taxation. A key reason for taxing a resident's worldwide net wealth is that it is the sum of taxpayers' assets, wherever they are located, that determines their ability to pay the wealth tax (IMF, 1996). In addition, a wealth tax imposed only on assets held domestically would encourage capital flight so a net wealth tax on worldwide assets of tax residents appears to be appropriate (Iara, 2015). With regard to non-residents, taxing assets that are located within the taxing jurisdiction (i.e. source-based taxation) might distort the international allocation of capital, although non-residents may be exempt from the wealth tax on financial investments made in the taxing jurisdiction (e.g. France). It is important to highlight that worldwide taxation for residents and source-based taxation for non-residents may lead to double taxation and therefore requires provisions preventing double taxation.

The scope of wealth taxes varies across countries. Both income and non-income generating assets are typically taxed under a net wealth tax. They can include land, real estate, bank accounts, bonds, shares, investment funds, life insurance policies, vehicles, boats, aircraft, jewellery, art and antiques, intellectual or industrial property rights, although different countries apply different exemptions and reliefs (Table 4.3).

As discussed below, net wealth tax bases are often narrowed by numerous exemptions and reliefs motivated by different rationales, the most important being enhancing fairness (e.g. for primary residences) and addressing social concerns (e.g. pension assets), liquidity issues (e.g. farm assets which may not generate sufficient income to enable the owner to pay the wealth tax), supporting entrepreneurship and investment (e.g. for business assets), avoiding valuation and other administration difficulties (e.g. artwork, jewellery, shares in unlisted businesses), and preserving countries' cultural heritage (e.g. artwork, antiques).

Pension assets typically get full relief under net wealth taxes. Among the countries that provided information in response to the questionnaire, all reported net wealth tax exemptions for pension assets. Exemptions for pension assets are justified on social grounds, because of the social benefits that come from retirement income, but also because it difficult to justify both socially and politically taxing individuals on wealth that is not within their present control and from which they cannot withdraw funds to pay the tax (Brown, 1991). However, this creates inequities between different taxpayers, raises fairness concerns, and creates tax planning opportunities.

The exemption for business assets has been justified as a way to encourage entrepreneurship and investment in productive assets, but it has not been universal. The countries that reported exemptions for business assets include France, Spain and Sweden. For the business asset exemption to apply, rules typically require that real economic activities are being performed (possibly excluding activities such as the management of movable or fixed assets, e.g. Spain), that the taxpayer performs a managing role, that income derived from the activity is the main source of the taxpayer's revenue and/or that the taxpayer owns a minimum percentage of shares in the company (e.g. 25% in France and Sweden; 5% in Spain). Other countries generally tax business assets but often grant tax preferences in the form of preferential valuation rules, the exemption of a proportion of assets, the exclusion of certain assets or a lower tax rate (e.g. Germany, Norway, Luxembourg and Ireland).

Other assets that are often exempt from net wealth taxes include artwork and antiques on the basis that they are difficult to value and help protect national heritage. Indeed, five countries reported exemptions for artwork and/or antiques. Exemptions for furniture and jewellery are less common, although some countries do exempt these assets. An alternative to a full exemption for personal and household effects is an exemption for assets below a certain value, particularly for household items such as furniture which are often of limited value.

Other assets, in particular main residences, are often taxed preferentially under net wealth taxes. Tax relief for owner-occupied housing is justified as a way to avoid burdening the middle class whose wealth mainly consists of the primary residence (see Chapter 2) but also because owner-occupied housing does not generate the income needed to pay the tax. However, preferential wealth tax treatment for the primary residence might induce shifts in investments away from productive activities towards residential property, especially if homeownership is already encouraged by other provisions in the tax system (e.g. no capital gains tax for primary residences). Tax relief often takes the form of tax allowances or preferential valuation rules. France and Spain offer tax allowances on the value of main residences, equal to 30% in France and up to EUR 300 000 in Spain. In Switzerland, as a general rule, housing is taxed at 60% of its market value. Norway offers a particularly favourable treatment for primary residences, which are valued at 25% of their estimated market value for net wealth tax purposes. In both Switzerland and Norway, these very favourable rules may be a way to compensate for the relatively low tax exemption thresholds, which imply that a portion of the middle or upper middle class are subject to net wealth taxes. Other assets also tend to benefit from a preferential tax treatment, including woods and forests, agricultural assets, small savings, life insurance policies, government bonds, charitable donations or investment in SMEs.

Table 4.3. Treatment of assets under net wealth taxes in 2017

Categories of assets	Assets	France	Norway	Spain	Switzerland	Austria (1994)	Germany (1997)	Finland (2006)	Ireland (1978)	Luxembourg (2006)	Netherlands (2001)	Sweden (2007)
Immovable property	Buildings	T	TP	T	TP	T	T	TP	T	T	T	T
	Main residence	TP	TP	TP	TP	T	×	TP	E	T	TP	T
	Woods and forests	TP	TP	TP	TP	T	T	TP	E	T	E	E
	Land	T	TP	T	TP	T	T	T	T	T	T	E
Movable property	Agricultural or rural assets	TP	TP	TP	TP	T	T	T	TP	T	T	E
	Furniture	T	TP	TP	E	T	×	E	T	T	E	E
	Artwork and antiques	E	TP	TP	TP	T	E	T	E	T	E	E
	Jewellery	T	TP	T	T	T	×	T	T	T	TP	E
	Vehicles	T	TP	T	TP	T	×	E	T	T	T	T
Financial assets	Shares	T	TP	TP	T	T	×	TP	T	TP	T	T
	Life insurance	T	E	T	T	T	×	E	×	T	E	T
	Bonds	T	T	T	T	T	×	E	T	T	T	T
	Liquidities	T	T	T	T	T	×	E	T	TP	T	T
	IP rights	T	E	E	T	T	E	E	×	E	T	E
	Pension savings	E	E	E	E	T	E	E	E	E	E	E
	Business assets	E	TP	E	TP	T	TP	T	TP	TP	TP	E

Note: T= fully taxed; E = full exemption; TP = tax preference; x: no information. No information for Denmark, Finland and Iceland.
Source: OECD Questionnaire on Current and Historical Net Wealth Taxes

In general, the tax base should be as broad as possible to avoid creating distortions in savings decisions as well as incentives and opportunities for tax avoidance. As mentioned in Chapter 3, tax exemptions and reliefs generate a number of issues: they reduce horizontal equity and create distortions in investment decisions; they tend to favour non-productive assets (e.g. housing, jewellery); they add to the system's complexity; they generate significant tax avoidance opportunities and ultimately work against the equity goals of wealth taxes as the wealthiest households are best able to shift the composition of their wealth towards untaxed assets. Exempting pension assets and household effects below a certain value may be justified, although if the overall tax exemption threshold is set at a sufficiently high level, many of these exemptions, in particular the ones aimed at addressing equity and social concerns, are not as necessary.

There is some justification for exempting business assets, but clear rules are needed to prevent abuse. As mentioned already, taxing business assets might deter investment in productive assets and generate valuation difficulties. However, exempting or providing significant relief for business assets creates tax avoidance opportunities, particularly at the very top of the wealth distribution, encouraging taxpayers to shelter their assets within their business. In fact, there is strong evidence that this mechanism is being used for tax avoidance purposes (see below). It is therefore critical to have clear criteria restricting the availability of this exemption, focusing on ensuring that real business activity is taking place and that assets are being directly used in the taxpayer's professional activity.

Debt deductibility

Net wealth taxes are levied on net assets, meaning that debts are deductible. As discussed in Chapter 3, from an equity perspective, it make sense to tax net wealth, as net wealth is a better reflection of taxpayers' ability to pay. However, debt deductibility provides incentives to borrow and can encourage tax avoidance. If the wealth tax base is narrow, taxpayers will have an incentive to avoid the tax by borrowing and investing in exempt assets or – if debt is only deductible when incurred to acquire taxable assets – taxpayers will have an incentive to invest part of their savings in tax-exempt assets and finance their savings in taxable assets through debt.

In practice, rules regarding debt deductibility have varied. Some countries have tried to limit tax avoidance opportunities by excluding debts incurred to acquire exempt assets from deductible liabilities (e.g. Austria, France, Germany, Spain and Sweden). For assets whose value is only partly included in the wealth tax base, rules have often been introduced to restrict the deductibility of debts incurred to acquire them. For instance, in France, only 25% of the debts incurred to acquire woods and forests, which are exempt from the net wealth tax for 75% of their value, are deductible.

Valuation rules

To ensure horizontal equity, valuation rules should be similar across assets and based on market values, but in practice valuation rules differ across assets and countries. Assets should ideally be assessed at their market value, defined as the price at which an asset would be traded in a competitive market. However, as mentioned in Chapter 3, one of the biggest practical difficulties with net wealth taxes is determining the value of infrequently traded assets. In some cases, these hard-to-value assets have been exempt. In addition, asset values need to be regularly updated which further increases administrative and compliance costs.

For housing property, market values are usually used. Most countries reported using estimated market values for immovable property. As discussed above, most countries provide tax relief in the form of discounted values for primary residences. In some cases, however, cadastral or fiscal values (i.e. valuation of properties in public registers used for tax purposes) may be used (e.g. Austria). In Spain, the tax base is calculated by taking the highest of three values: the cadastral value used as a basis for the recurrent tax on immovable property, the value assessed by tax authorities for the purpose of other taxes, or the purchase price. Importantly, there can be discrepancies between the housing values used for recurrent taxes on immovable property taxes and those used for net wealth taxes, in particular when the former are based on cadastral values while the latter are based on estimated market values. For instance, in France, while market value is used for net wealth tax purposes, the recurrent tax on immovable property (*taxe foncière*) is based on cadastral rental values.

Regarding securities which are listed on a stock exchange, approaches are relatively similar. Countries typically use closing stock market values or the average trading price in the period preceding the end of the year (e.g. last 30 trading days in France, last quarter in Spain). In France, taxpayers can choose between the two options (i.e. last quoted price or average trading price in the last 30 trading days). Using average values may be a better option as they can take into account fluctuations.

Valuation is of course more difficult in the case of unlisted shares and approaches differ. Valuing unincorporated businesses and unquoted shares raises difficulties. An important consideration is whether goodwill should be included in the valuation of business assets, or alternatively, whether businesses should simply be valued on the aggregate value of their physical assets. Of course, merely taking the book value of assets substantially understates the value of a business (McDonnell, 2013; Rudnick and Gordon, 1996). There are also issues related to the estimation of a business' stock of physical assets. In practice, approaches have differed. In France, there are three methods for unlisted companies: the mathematical value after the revaluation of assets, the value of the return according to distributed profits, and the value of productivity. As a general rule, the valuation of the company will result from a combination of these different values. In Spain, the book value from the last audited balance sheet is used for the valuation of shares in unquoted companies. If the balance sheet has not been verified or has received a negative audit report, however, they are valued at the highest of: (i) the face value; (ii) the theoretical value resulting from the last balance sheet or (iii) the value resulting from capitalisation at 20% of the average profits of the three financial years before the tax becomes chargeable. Overall, irrespective of the methodology used, a uniform approach is needed for administrative purposes and taxpayer certainty (McDonnell, 2013).

As mentioned in Chapter 3, the date of valuation can also raise issues. If assets are valued on 1 January, then the net wealth tax is partly levied on wealth that will be consumed later in the year. This distorts the timing of consumption decisions as taxpayers will have an incentive to bring their consumption forward to the end of the previous year. This argument is less convincing, however, if the net wealth tax base is broad. A lot of consumption occurring at the top of the wealth distribution actually consists in buying assets that would be taxed under a broad-based net wealth tax (e.g. cars, jewellery, artwork). On the other hand, if assets are valued at the end of the year, taxpayers may be taxed on wealth that they have accumulated during the year which implies that savings would be taxed twice in the same year. In practice, valuation dates have varied, with some countries using as a general rule values on 1 January (e.g. France), and others using as a general rule values at the end of the year (e.g. Spain, Sweden, Switzerland).

In general, asset valuations should be based on market values, possibly at a slightly discounted rate, and valuation rules should be kept simple. While assets should be assessed at their market value, the tax base could be limited to a fixed percentage of that market value (e.g. 80-85%) to prevent valuation disputes but also to take into account certain costs that may be incurred to hold or maintain the assets. The rules should nevertheless be comparable across asset classes to avoid generating large distortions between assets. For assets that are infrequently traded and therefore hard-to-value, including artwork and high-value jewellery, insured values can be used instead of market values. There are also a number of ways to simplify asset valuations. In some cases, values for specific asset classes could be treated as fixed for a few years (e.g. France in the case of furniture, where estimated value is valid for three years). Alternatively, the value of taxpayers' total net wealth could be treated as fixed for a few years before being re-assessed (McDonnell, 2013). As is often the case, valuation rules that are used for other taxes, in particular for taxes on residential property and inheritances, can be used for net wealth tax purposes as well. Finally, if values are assessed at a specific date, rules should be put in place to prevent abuse aiming at artificially lowering the value of assets just before the valuation date.

Tax rates

Net wealth tax rates and rate structures have varied across countries, but a majority of countries have applied flat tax rates. The lowest marginal tax rates have generally ranged between less than 0.2% and 1.5%, while the top marginal rates have generally varied between 0.5% and 2.5% (McDonnell, 2013). Spain has the highest top net wealth tax rate, at 2.5%, which applies to income above EUR 10 695 996. Tax rate structures have also varied across countries. Among the countries covered in this chapter, a majority of countries reported flat tax rates including Austria, Germany, Ireland, Luxembourg, the Netherlands, Norway and Sweden. On the other hand, France, Spain and a majority of Swiss cantons apply progressive tax rates that rise with total net wealth (Figure 4.2).

In countries where wealth taxes are local taxes, tax rates can vary quite significantly across municipalities or local governments. In Switzerland, there is considerable variation in wealth tax rates across cantons. In 2012, top wealth tax rates varied by a factor of almost 8, ranging from 0.13% to 1.0%, with the highest rates being levied in the Western French-speaking cantons and the lowest rates found in the small German-speaking cantons of central Switzerland (Brülhart et al., 2017). In Spain, there is a general tax rate schedule at the level of the central government, but the autonomous regions have room to determine their own tax scales. Top tax rates, for instance, vary across regions (e.g. 3.03% in Andalucía, 3% in Murcia, and 2.75% in Cataluña) (Durán-Cabré, 2017).

There has generally been a decrease in tax rates since the 2000s. In Switzerland, there has been a general downward trend in net wealth tax rates, but with wide variations across cantons. Tax cuts have been most significant in the central cantons, where tax competition was vigorous in the early 2000s; but other cantons have also significantly reduced their wealth tax rates. The high-tax western cantons, on the other hand, have not seen much change in their wealth tax rates (Brülhart et al., 2017). In France as well, the top tax rate in 2017 was lower than in the early 2000s. In 2011, the net wealth tax was reformed, with a simplification of the tax rate schedule and a reduction in the top tax rate from 1.80% to 0.50%. The following year, however, a new reform was introduced increasing the number of brackets and lifting the top tax rate to 1.50%. More recently, in Norway, the tax rate was lowered from 1.1% in 2013 to 0.85%, as part of a broader effort to reduce the wealth tax burden (accompanied by progressive increases in the tax exemption threshold and changes in the assessment rules) to promote Norwegian ownership and investment in business assets. In Spain, on the other hand, the Central government tax rate schedule has not changed since 2002.

Figure 4.2. Bottom and top net wealth tax rates in 2017 or in the latest year of operation

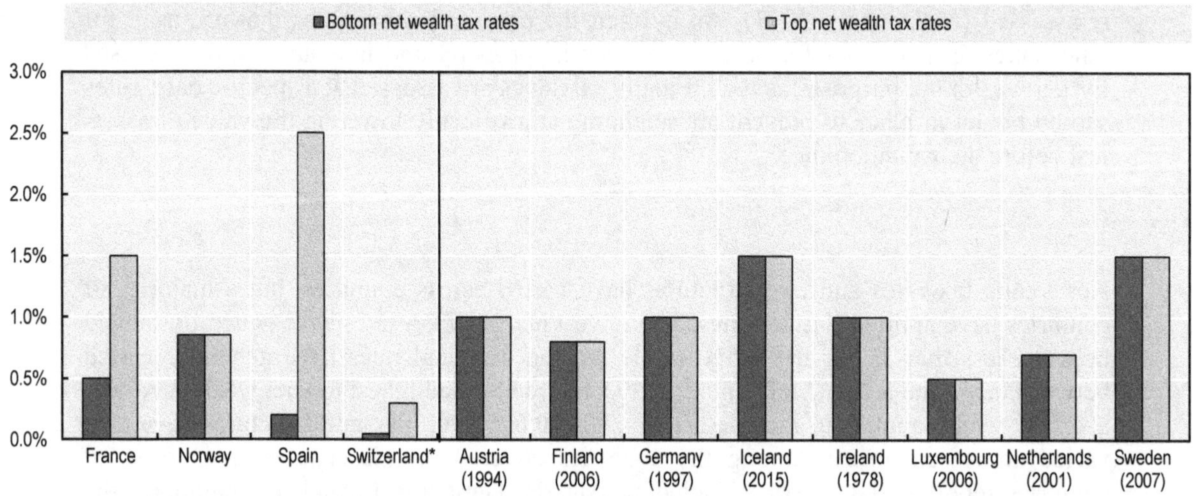

Note: * In Switzerland, tax rates in the canton of Zurich. No information for Denmark.
Source: OECD Questionnaire on Current and Historical Net Wealth Taxes

Overall, net wealth tax rates should be low, especially as this report also recommends maintaining a broad tax base. A low tax rate will limit the overall tax burden on capital, which tends to be particularly high when a wealth tax is imposed on top of taxes on capital income. Tax rates should also preferably be progressive to ensure greater equity, in particular given the fact that a flat net wealth tax would penalise the holders of low-return assets who tend to be less wealthy than the holders of high-return assets. Countries could also implement inflation-adjusted net wealth tax rates, which would mean that in high inflation environments, tax rates would be lower. The idea is that the tax would be as much as possible levied on real imputed returns, i.e. excluding the return that compensates for inflation.

Caps on total tax liability

Ceiling provisions or tax caps are common features of net wealth taxes. These often consist in setting a limit to the combined total of net wealth tax and personal income tax liability as a maximum share of income. They are used to prevent unreasonably high tax burdens and liquidity constraints requiring assets to be sold to pay the net wealth tax. In France, the wealth tax ceiling (often referred to as the "*bouclier fiscal*") limits total French and foreign taxes to 75% of taxpayers' total income. If the percentage is exceeded, the surplus is deducted from the wealth tax. In Spain, the aggregate burden of income tax and net wealth tax due by a resident taxpayer may not exceed 60% of their total taxable income. If it exceeds that amount, taxpayers may reduce their net wealth tax liability by the excess amount. However, Spain also has a floor provision requiring that a minimum of 20% of the net wealth tax liability, as originally calculated, be paid. In Switzerland, some but not all cantons have similar ceiling provisions. Indeed, seven (of the 26) cantons have limitation rules based either on the net rent of net wealth, a limit of wealth tax payments as a share of total taxable income or a limit of wealth tax payments as a share of total net wealth. Norway, on the other hand, does not have a tax cap.

In practice, these tax caps, in addition to lowering potential revenues from net wealth taxes, create significant opportunities for tax avoidance. These caps encourage taxpayers to engage in tax planning to minimise their income, which then allows them to reduce their wealth tax burden through the tax cap. Safeguards should therefore be put in place to avoid tax planning through tax caps (see below).

Tax caps also have real effects that need to be taken into account. For taxpayers with a fixed income level whose tax liability is at or above the tax cap (e.g. total of their income and wealth tax liability equal to or above 75% of their income), owning more wealth does not result in more tax liability. For taxpayers with a fixed level of wealth whose tax liability is at or above the tax cap, however, an increase in income, which will raise the nominal amount of the tax cap, will not only cause an increase in the income tax liability but will also raise the wealth tax liability, thereby generating a strong disincentive to earn more income either through work or other income-generating activities.

Tax filing and payment procedures

Wealth tax filing is generally based on self-assessment. This means that each household is responsible for assessing whether or not they are liable to pay the tax. Tax authorities can of course decide to investigate and audit households to ensure compliance and where taxpayers have not properly self-assessed their tax liability collect tax arrears and/or apply penalties. Nevertheless, relying on self-assessment makes non-disclosure or underreporting – deliberate or not – more likely. This differs from withholding at source and third-party reporting which are well-developed for many forms of capital income taxation such as dividends and interest, although in theory the same tools could be put in place for the taxation of capital stocks (Keen, 2014). In addition to risks of non-disclosure and underreporting, self-assessment imposes a significant compliance burden on taxpayers (Brown, 1991).

Nevertheless, tax filing procedures differ across countries. In most countries, taxpayers have to file a separate wealth tax return (i.e. separate from the income tax return). However, wealth tax returns may be consolidated with income tax returns. In France, if net taxable assets are between EUR 1.3 and 2.57 million, taxpayers do not have to file a separate wealth tax return; assets have to be reported on the income tax return. Above EUR 2.57 million of total net wealth, taxpayers are required to file a separate wealth tax return. In Norway and Switzerland, the wealth tax return is also consolidated with the income tax return.

Regarding tax payment procedures, specific wealth tax provisions allowing payment deferral or payments in instalments are rare. As discussed in Chapter 3, liquidity issues are one of the biggest concerns related to net wealth taxes. Ways to address this issue include provisions allowing for payments to be made in instalments or for payment deferral until assets are sold. Such provisions are rare in practice, although some countries may have general tax rules (i.e. that do not apply specifically to wealth taxes) allowing tax payment deferral or payments in instalments (e.g. Spain).

A few good practices may help enhance tax filing accuracy as well as lower administrative and compliance costs. Concerning tax filing, even if the wealth and income tax returns are separate, it may be good to require both tax returns to be filed at the same time, which would allow wealth tax returns to be cross-checked with income tax returns to verify consistency and obtain information that may be relevant in auditing both taxes (Rudnick and Gordon, 1996). With regard to tax payments, measures allowing payment deferral until assets are sold could be envisaged, although they could generate lock-in effects. A better option would be to allow tax payments in instalments. This type of relief – allowing taxes to be paid over multiple years at a very low interest rate – could be granted to specific categories of taxpayers (e.g. self-employed businesses, farms) or be based on the composition of taxpayers' assets (Rudnick and Gordon, 1996).

Anti-avoidance/evasion rules

A major concern with net wealth taxes is the ability of wealthier taxpayers to avoid or evade the tax. This has limited the potential of net wealth taxes to achieve their redistributive objectives and has contributed to perceptions of unfairness. This sub-section examines the most common forms of tax avoidance and evasion that countries have faced as well as measures that have been adopted to prevent them.

Different tax avoidance and evasion strategies have been widely used, some of them encouraged by the mobility of financial capital, others by some of the design features of net wealth taxes. The most common forms of avoidance and evasion reported by surveyed countries include using tax shelters available to the wealthiest such as vehicles to conceal the beneficial ownership of assets, avoidance through the exemption for business assets, avoidance through tax cap provisions, avoidance through other tax preferences provided under net wealth taxes, and finally simply holding assets abroad and not declaring them to tax authorities.

Avoidance/evasion through trusts

As discussed in Chapter 3, although they can be set up for perfectly legitimate reasons, trusts can also potentially be used to avoid taxes on net wealth and wealth transfers since they confer the benefits of wealth without transferring the legal ownership of the property. Indeed, they are often used to separate the entitlement to the income that property generates from the entitlement to the property itself (Adam et al., 2011). Thus, rules are needed to prevent tax avoidance through the use of trusts.

Trusts have been problematic in civil law countries which do not recognise them. Indeed, the fact that civil law countries do not recognise trusts has generated uncertainty regarding the taxation of assets held in trusts. In France, there was a significant change in 2011 regarding the wealth tax treatment of trust assets requiring that all assets and rights be included in the settlor's estate – unless the settlor is deceased, in which case the beneficiaries are subject to the tax on trust assets. Spain has adopted a similar approach, although it is not specified in the tax code. According to the Spanish tax authorities, it is also understood that settlors (or beneficiaries when the effective transfer is considered to occur, for example, upon the settlor's death) are subject to the wealth tax with respect to assets held in a trust. In that sense, trusts are disregarded and transactions carried out through trusts are considered as if they were direct transactions effected directly between settlors and beneficiaries, even if trustees have discretionary powers on the management and allocation of assets (Vidal Wagner and García-Perrote Forn, 2012).

Indeed, treating trusts as "see-through" entities seems appropriate. Following the approaches adopted in France and Spain, trusts can be treated as transparent or "see-through" in the sense that the trustee is legally obligated to identify the settlor or beneficiary/ies to tax authorities with the value of assets held in the trusts and then allocate these assets to the settlor or to the beneficiaries on a proportional basis to their assessable wealth (McDonnell, 2013).

Avoidance through the exemption for business assets

The exemption for business assets creates significant tax avoidance opportunities. In Spain, for instance, the government introduced a net wealth tax exemption for the shares of owner-managers in 1994. The exemption applied to business owners substantially involved in the management of their business, who individually owned at least 15% of the business (or with their families at least 20% of the business), and who received over 50% of their labour and business income from this activity. Looking at this exemption, Alvaredo and Saez (2009) showed that it progressively and substantially eroded the wealth tax base. Their empirical results reveal strong shifting effects whereby wealthy business owners re-organised their activities to take advantage of the exemption. In 2003, the rules of the exemption were modified, only requiring an individual stock ownership of 5%. Looking at the reintroduction of the Spanish wealth tax in 2011, Durán-Cabré et al. (2017) also find evidence that taxpayers who declared business ownership in 2011 were more responsive to wealth taxes. This suggests that taxpayers transfer part of their wealth in real estate, bank accounts and non-exempted business holdings to exempted business holdings, which is relatively easy once the business structure is set up (Durán-Cabré et al., 2017).

As mentioned already, there is some justification for the exemption of business assets, but clear rules are needed to prevent abuse. Given that there is strong evidence that this exemption is being used for tax avoidance purposes, it is critical to have clear criteria restricting the availability of this exemption. Requirements for the business asset exemption to apply should focus in particular on ensuring that real business activity is taking place and that assets are being used directly in the taxpayer's professional activity. Businesses whose main activity consists in managing movable or real assets could also be excluded to prevent abuse (e.g. Spain).

Avoidance through tax caps

Tax caps can be used as a tax avoidance mechanism. As discussed above, tax caps generally impose a limit on a taxpayer's total tax liability as a share of their income. There are various strategies that taxpayers can use to reduce their taxable income and thereby ultimately minimise their wealth tax liability. For instance, in France, taxpayers can reduce their income by investing in life insurance policies. If a taxpayer holds a large sum of cash on bank deposit accounts, the money will be included in the wealth tax calculation along with the value of other assets. The interest earned will also be considered as income and subject to PIT. If those savings are placed in an *assurance vie* and left there, however, the value of insurance policies will generally be taken into account in wealth tax calculations but savings will not be considered as generating income until withdrawal. This minimises income, which in turn can be used, through the tax cap, to lower the wealth tax bill. Another mechanism to reduce taxable income – and ultimately the wealth tax liability through the tax cap – is to capitalise cash in a financial holding entity. In the 2017 Budget Law, France sought to target this so called "cash box" practice by enabling tax authorities to capture artificially capitalised income for the computation of the wealth tax ceiling, provided that they can prove that this was done to avoid the wealth tax (PWC, 2017).

Tax caps may be justified to limit taxpayers' overall tax burdens as well as to address liquidity issues. Tax caps may be relevant for taxpayers facing liquidity constraints, as is likely to be the case for retirees, farmers or new businesses. As shown in Chapter 3, METRs including net wealth taxes can also reach very high levels, especially when the rates of return from households' assets are low, which may also justify capping taxpayers' total tax liability as a share of their income. To limit tax avoidance and the wealth tax liability potentially being reduced to zero, however, tax caps could be accompanied by a floor provision which limits the amount of relief provided by the tax cap (McDonnell, 2013), as is the case in Spain. More generally, strategies to minimise income should be prevented in order to reduce tax avoidance through tax caps.

However, as discussed already, tax caps also have real effects that need to be taken into account and it may be argued that if net wealth taxes are properly designed, tax caps are not as necessary. First, if the exemption threshold is set at a sufficiently high level, liquidity issues become less significant, in particular as liquidity constraints are mostly related to real property. In addition, as mentioned already, instalment relief, allowing the tax to be paid over multiple years at a very low interest rate, could be provided to specific categories of taxpayers including self-employed businesses and farms to limit liquidity issues. Liquidity constraints may also be less problematic than often thought as there is evidence that retirees dis-save or sell their assets to consume (see Chapter 2).

Hiding assets abroad

The combination of increasing capital mobility and the lack of transparency has also encouraged tax evasion, with taxpayers holding assets abroad and not declaring them to tax authorities. The increasing mobility of financial assets as well as the rise of tax havens, combined with the development of information and communication technology and the elimination of barriers to cross-border capital transfers (such as capital controls), have allowed taxpayers to move their capital offshore without declaring it and made the enforcement of capital income taxes and wealth taxes much more difficult (Krenek and Schratzenstaller, 2017). In fact, capital mobility has been a major factor behind the reduction of taxes on capital in the last few decades.

Estimations of offshore wealth, although challenging to calculate, confirm the existence of widespread tax evasion. Recent estimates in the literature have varied from USD 6-7 trillion to USD 22 trillion (Alstadsaeter, Johannesen and Zucman, 2017). Alstadsaeter et al. (2017) estimate that globally the equivalent of about 10% of the world GDP is held offshore, but that this average masks significant heterogeneity—from limited levels in Scandinavia, to about 15% in Continental Europe, and more than 50% in Russia, some Latin American countries, and Gulf countries. The general order of magnitude of these estimates suggests that levying residence-based personal taxes is a considerable policy challenge.

The recent progress made on international tax transparency and the exchange of information is enhancing countries' capabilities to tax capital effectively. International cooperation on the exchange of information on request (EOIR) and on the automatic exchange of information (AEOI) as well as in areas like beneficial ownership will reduce opportunities for tax evasion and ultimately allow countries to tax both capital and capital income more effectively. However, such efforts need to take into account that high-wealth individuals can change their tax residence and even their citizenship in response to high taxes and that, by limiting opportunities for tax avoidance and evasion, the real effects of taxes on capital – in particular on savings and investment – may be stronger (see above).

There will also be challenges to ensure that information exchange is effectively implemented. It will be critical to ensure that a comprehensive EOI network develops amongst all relevant jurisdictions and that persons, assets, and institutions not covered under existing EOI standards do not offer opportunities for continued tax evasion and thus frustrate the purpose of EOI. It is also important that peer review and technical support are ongoing, particularly for countries and jurisdictions with limited administrative capacity. The other challenge relates to coherently taxing capital income in a world where EOI is effectively implemented. First, the impact of EOI will be limited unless tax authorities have the means and methods to effectively use the information exchanged. Tax authorities should take advantage of new analytical tools and technological advances. The expansion and effectiveness of EOI may also induce taxpayers to shift their wealth towards assets that are not covered by the exchange of information, such as real property. This further stresses the importance of expanding the exchange of information to these assets.

Political economy considerations

The popularity of wealth taxes has varied across countries. Responses to the Net Wealth Tax Questionnaire reveal that wealth taxes were unpopular in a number of countries, which contributed to their repeal. However, experiences in other countries show that they have not been unpopular everywhere. In France, opinion polls have consistently shown a majority of respondents to be favourable to the net wealth tax. Recent evidence, based on online surveys in the United States, also reveals respondents' preference for positive wealth taxation (Fisman et al., 2017).

Differences in the popularity of wealth taxes may partly come from differences in awareness regarding capital income and wealth inequality. Bastani and Waldenström (forthcoming) explore whether information about capital inequality affects attitudes towards capital taxes through a survey sent to a representative sample of 12 000 Swedish adults in which they expose different parts of the target population to different information treatments regarding the distribution of capital income. One group receives special information about housing wealth, one receives special information about inherited fortunes, and the last group does not receive any special information at all. Because of the random assignment of individuals into these three groups, differences in attitudes between the different groups can be interpreted as a causal effect of this information. A similar argument may be made for inheritance taxes – i.e. addressing the lack of information on the inter-generational persistence of wealth gaps may help make these taxes more politically acceptable – although the unpopularity of inheritance taxes comes primarily from their salience and unfortunate timing.

In addition, the way wealth tax reforms are packaged is likely to affect how taxpayers view these taxes. If the introduction of a wealth tax or an increase in the existing wealth tax is part of a more comprehensive tax reform and goes hand-in-hand with a decrease in other taxes, especially in labour taxes which almost everyone is subject to, it may be more acceptable politically. Packaging a wealth tax reform as part of broader reform aiming at tax mix shifts as opposed to overall tax burden increases may increase the chances of the reform being adopted.

Box 4.2. Net wealth tax design recommendations

- Low tax rates, especially if the net wealth tax comes on top of capital income taxes;
- Progressive tax rates;
- Limited tax exemptions and reliefs;
- An exemption for business assets, with clear criteria restricting the availability of the exemption (ensuring that real business activity is taking place and that assets are directly being used in the taxpayer's professional activity)
- An exemption for personal and household effects up to a certain value;
- Determining the tax base based on asset market values; although the tax base could amount to a fixed percentage of that market value (e.g. 80-85%) to prevent valuation disputes and take into account costs that may be incurred to hold or maintain the assets
- Keeping the value of hard-to-value assets or the value of taxpayers' total net wealth constant for a few years to avoid yearly reassessments;
- Allowing debts to be deductible only if they have been incurred to acquire taxable assets – or, if the tax exemption threshold is high, consider further limiting debt deductibility;
- Measures allowing payments in instalments for taxpayers facing liquidity constraints;
- Ensuring transparency in the treatment of assets held in trusts;
- Continued efforts to enhance tax transparency and exchange information on the assets that residents hold in other jurisdictions;
- Developing third-party reporting;
- Establishing rules to prevent international double wealth taxation; and
- Regularly evaluating the effects of the wealth tax

Notes

[1] As mentioned, this chapter is based on the tax rules that were in place as of 1 September 2017. Since then, France has replaced its net wealth tax ("*impôt de solidarité sur la fortune*") with a new real estate wealth tax ("*impôt sur la fortune immobilière*"), with effect from 1 January 2018.

[2] The figure includes some double counting when taxpayers own wealth in more than one canton.

References

Alstadsaeter, A., Johannesen, N. and G. Zucman (2017), Tax Evasion and Inequality, Mimeo.

Boadway, R., Chamberlain E. and Emmerson C. (2010): "Taxation of Wealth and Wealth Transfers", In J. A. Mirrlees, S. Adam, T. Besley, R. Blundell, S. Bond, R. Chote, M. Gammie, P. Johnson, G. Myles and J. Poterba, eds., Dimensions of Tax Design: the Mirrlees Review, 8:737-836, Oxford University Press.

Brown, R. D. (1991), "A Primer on the Implementation of Wealth Taxes", Canadian Public Policy / Analyse de Politiques, Vol. 17, No. 3, pp. 335-350.

Brülhart, M., Gruber, J., Krapf, M. and K. Schmidheiny (2017), "Taxing Wealth: Evidence from Switzerland", NBER Working Paper Series, No. 22376.

Brys, B., et al. (2016), "Tax Design for Inclusive Economic Growth", OECD Taxation Working Papers, No. 26, OECD Publishing, Paris.

Durán-Cabré, J.M., Esteller-Moré, A. and M. Mas-Montserrat (2017), "Behavioural Responses to the (Re)Introduction of Wealth Taxes: Evidence from Spain", preliminary version.

Fisman, R., Gladstone, K., Kuziemko, I. and S. Naidu (2017), "Do Americans Want to Tax Capital? Evidence from Online Surveys", Washington Center for Equitable Growth, Washington D.C.

Iara, A. (2015), "Wealth Distribution and Taxation in EU Members", Taxation Papers, Working Paper No. 60, Brussels.

Keen, M. (2014), "Taxing Wealth: Policy Challenges and Recent Debates", presentation for the ECFIN Taxation Workshop - Taxing Wealth: Past, Present, Future, 13 November 2014.

Krenek, A. and M. Schratzenstaller (2017), "Sustainability-oriented Future EU Funding: A European Net Wealth Tax", FairTax WP-Series, No.10.

Lawless, M. and D. Lynch (2016), "Scenarios and Distributional Implications of a Household Wealth Tax in Ireland", ESRI Working Paper, No.549.

McDonnell, T.A. (2013), "Wealth Tax: Options for its Implementation in the Republic of Ireland", NERI Working Paper Series, WP 2013/6.

Norwegian Ministry of Finance (2017), "The Norwegian Tax System - Main Features and Developments", Chapter 2 of the Budget Proposal on Taxes 2017: https://www.statsbudsjettet.no/upload/Statsbudsjett_2017/dokumenter/pdf/main_features_tax_system.pdf

OECD (2018), Taxation of Household Savings, Tax Policy Studies, OECD Publishing, Paris.

OECD (2010), Tax Policy Reform and Economic Growth, OECD Publishing, Paris. http://dx.doi.org/10.1787/9789264091085-en

PWC (2017), "2017 French Finance Bill Individual Tax: Major provisions", available at https://www.pwcavocats.com/fr/ealertes/ealertes-international/2017-french-finance-bill-individual tax-major-provisions.html

Schnellenbach, J. (2012), "The Economics of Taxing Net Wealth: A Survey of the Issues", Freiburger Diskussionspapiere zur Ordnungsokonomik, No. 12/5.

Vidal Wagner, G. and M. García-Perrote Forn (2012), "Spanish Tax Treatment for Foreign Trusts", The Journal of International *Tax, Trust and Corporate Planning* Vol. 19, No.3.

Chapter 5. Conclusions and policy implications

This chapter highlights the main conclusions of the report regarding the role of the tax system in addressing wealth inequality and whether a net wealth tax is the most appropriate instrument to achieve that objective. It also provides a number of practical tax design recommendations for countries that already have or wish to implement net wealth taxes.

This report has attempted to answer four key questions:

- Is there a rationale for addressing wealth inequality through the tax system?
- If so, is a net wealth tax the most appropriate instrument to address wealth inequality?
- What have been the practical experiences of countries that currently have or have previously had net wealth taxes?
- And where a country has decided to implement a net wealth tax, how should it be designed to maximise efficiency and equity and minimise tax administration and compliance costs?

This report argues that there is a strong case for addressing wealth inequality through the tax system. Wealth inequality is far greater than income inequality, and there is some evidence suggesting that wealth inequality has increased in recent decades. In addition, wealth accumulation operates in a self-reinforcing way and is likely to increase in the absence of taxation. High earners are able to save more, meaning that they are able to invest more and ultimately accumulate more wealth. Moreover, investment returns tend to increase with wealth. Wealthy taxpayers, who tend to have more diversified asset holdings, are in a better position to invest in riskier assets which will tend to generate higher returns. The ability of the wealthiest taxpayers to generate higher average returns may also come from their higher level of financial education as well as their access to financial expertise and more lucrative investment opportunities. Rich taxpayers are also more likely to obtain loans, which will in turn allow them to invest more and accumulate more wealth. Finally, it may be argued that wealth may confer more power, which may ultimately beget more wealth.

There are many channels through which tax systems can affect wealth inequality. Sources of wealth inequality are diverse. The most significant ones include income inequality, inheritances and asset value appreciation. This means that a broad range of taxes will affect wealth inequality. In addition to net wealth taxes, taxes on wealth transfers, labour and capital income taxes, and capital gains taxes can have an impact on the distribution of wealth. Therefore, the question is whether a net wealth tax is the most appropriate tax policy option, among those that are available, to address wealth inequality. The most appropriate tax policies are those that minimise equity and efficiency trade-offs and involve comparatively lower tax administration and compliance costs.

While reducing wealth concentration at the top is essential, it will not be enough to reduce wealth inequality. Supporting wealth accumulation by households with medium or low levels of wealth is also critical to narrowing wealth gaps, which implies that the design of taxes on capital or on capital income should not discourage households in the middle or at the bottom of the wealth distribution from saving. This also highlights the need to use policy tools beyond taxation to address wealth inequality. In some countries, wealth inequality has been explained, among other factors, by differences in saving rates and investment returns, with lower saving rates and investment returns at the bottom of the wealth distribution, resulting in a decline in the share of wealth held by the poorer segments of the population. Therefore, measures supporting savings at the bottom of the income and wealth distribution as well as financial education to inform lower income and wealth individuals about investment opportunities yielding higher returns can play an important role in addressing wealth inequality.

Overall, the report suggests that from both an efficiency and equity perspective, there are limited arguments for having a net wealth tax on top of broad-based personal capital income taxes and well-designed inheritance and gift taxes. However, there are stronger arguments for having a net wealth tax in the absence of broad-based capital income taxes and taxes on wealth transfers. Where the overall tax burden on capital is low or where levying broad-based capital income taxes or an inheritance tax is not feasible – net wealth taxes may play an important (albeit imperfect) substitution role.

While net wealth taxes can to some extent be compared to taxes on capital income, there are a number of features that clearly distinguish them. A first key difference is that a net wealth tax is equivalent to a proportional tax on a presumptive return, meaning that the tax is levied irrespective of the actual returns earned on savings. A second significant difference is that a wealth tax is in theory levied on an accrual basis while income taxes are typically levied upon realisation. Another major difference is that a net wealth tax can potentially be more comprehensive than a capital income tax, covering both income and non-income generating assets.

The equivalence of a net wealth tax with a proportional tax on a presumptive return has negative efficiency implications. As discussed in Chapter 3, a tax on the stock of wealth is equivalent to taxing a presumptive return but exempting returns above that presumptive return. Where the presumptive return is set at the level of or at a level close to the normal - or risk-free – return to savings, a wealth tax is economically equivalent to a tax on the normal return to savings, which is considered to be inefficient. Indeed, the taxation of normal returns is likely to distort the timing of consumption and ultimately the decision to save, as the normal return is what compensates for delays in consumption (Mirrlees et al., 2011).

Taxing a presumptive return may encourage a more productive use of assets, but this argument has limitations. The argument is that wealth taxes do not discourage investment *per se* but discourage investments in low-yielding assets and reinforce the incentives to invest in higher-yielding assets because there is an additional cost to holding assets, which is not linked to the return they generate. However, higher returns do not always mean higher productivity and efficiency. There may be cases where asset returns do not reflect higher productivity and where recurrent net wealth taxes may therefore not support an efficient allocation of resources. For instance, above-market returns may be the result of luck or privileged market access. Favouring high returns may also discourage potentially highly profitable investments, such as investments in start-ups which are likely to generate low returns in their early stages.

Taxing a presumptive return also has negative equity implications. As net wealth taxes are equivalent to taxing a presumptive return, the effective tax rate decreases when actual returns increase. This may have negative equity effects. Indeed, as mentioned above, there is evidence of heterogeneous returns that are positively correlated with wealth. This means that if the wealth tax applies to (part of) the middle class, it might have regressive effects. For instance, taxpayers with a large portion of their assets in regular savings accounts, for which the rate of return is close to zero, are taxed for a return they generally did not realise, while wealthier taxpayers who have invested a lot of their savings in shares tend to realise higher gains than they are taxed for.

Nevertheless, a net wealth tax can be designed to be progressive. Despite inequities that arise from the taxation of a presumptive return, a wealth tax can be levied at progressive rates and/or different presumptive returns which increase with household wealth can be used. A high wealth tax exemption threshold can also create a significant amount of tax progressivity, even under a proportional tax rate.

As mentioned above, another major characteristic of net wealth taxes is that they are in theory levied on an accrual basis, which has positive efficiency effects. Under the assumption that the wealth tax base is kept up to date through regular asset valuations, the appreciation in asset values is taxed every year under a wealth tax. This differs from income taxes which are typically levied upon realisation. Accrual-based taxation does not create lock-in effects and the resulting inefficiencies in capital allocation. Indeed, under a wealth tax, there is no tax-induced incentive to defer the realisation of capital gains and to bring forward the realisation of capital losses to benefit from their tax deductibility (if any).

However, accrual-based taxation has mixed equity implications and involves significant practical challenges. As the net wealth tax has to be paid irrespective of actual returns, taxpayers may face liquidity issues when the tax has to be paid, especially if part of their wealth cannot be converted into liquid funds and if they cannot rely on alternative sources of income. On the other hand, tax liabilities will in theory be less affected by taxpayers' tax planning strategies and will therefore be more equitable across taxpayers. Accrual-based taxation also involves significant practical challenges, in particular related to the valuation of taxable assets.

An alternative could be to levy capital income taxes upon accrual. Under a mark-to-market tax, the increase in wealth would be taxed upon accrual. Such an approach would limit some of the tax arbitrage opportunities that exist in current capital income tax systems in OECD countries. An in-depth discussion of these issues could be the focus of future work.

Net wealth taxes can be levied on broad bases, although in practice numerous exemptions and reliefs have narrowed tax bases. As opposed to capital income taxes, under a net wealth tax, even the assets that do not generate monetary returns are generally taxed. For instance, artworks which increase their owner's wellbeing but do not generate any monetary returns until they are sold are often (at least partly) included in the tax base. In practice, however, these assets have often been excluded from net wealth tax bases because they are hard to value, easy to underreport or hide, and lead to liquidity difficulties.

Finally, when they are levied on top of capital income taxes, net wealth taxes can result in very high overall tax burdens on personal capital. When net wealth taxes have to be paid on top of capital income taxes, overall tax burdens on personal capital can reach very high levels, with METRs sometimes reaching values close to or above 100% in some countries. In addition to their discouraging effects on savings and investment, very high overall tax burdens on capital may encourage wealthy taxpayers to adjust their wealth portfolio, engage in tax planning or evasion, or change their tax residence to minimise their wealth tax liability.

Overall, broad-based capital income taxes tend to be a more efficient and less administratively costly way of taxing capital. To strengthen progressivity, the way countries tax personal capital income could be revisited. In particular, progressive rates could be applied to personal capital income. As argued in previous OECD work (Brys et al., 2016), countries could consider introducing "dual progressive income tax" systems which would tax capital income under a separate rate schedule at progressive rates. The rate schedule could exempt or tax at low rates total household capital income below a minimum threshold. This could also encourage taxpayers at the bottom of the income and wealth distribution to save more, which could ultimately contribute to reducing wealth inequality. Finally, as mentioned above, consideration could be given to taxing capital gains upon accrual, noting the practical difficulties of doing so.

Inheritance taxes are also central to addressing the persistence of wealth gaps from one generation to the next and tend to be less distortive than net wealth taxes. The report argues that capital income taxes alone will most likely not be enough to address wealth inequality and suggests the need to complement capital income taxes with a form of wealth taxation. The report finds that there is a strong case for an accompanying inheritance tax. The double taxation argument, often raised against net wealth taxes, is weaker in the case of inheritance taxes, as there is no double taxation of the donor and the inherited wealth is also only taxed once in the hands of the recipient. Effects on savings are also likely to be smaller than in the case of recurrent taxes on personal net wealth, and empirically they have generally been found to be negative but small. Inheritance taxes are also easier to administer and comply with as they are only levied once. Finally, and perhaps more importantly, there are meritocratic arguments for taxing inherited wealth more than self-made wealth. However, further work is needed to determine how to design inheritance taxes in a way that makes them both more efficient and fairer.

However, this report also argues that, in countries where the taxation of capital income – including capital gains – is low or where inheritance taxes are not levied, there is a stronger case for a net wealth tax. Brys et al. (2016) have argued for the need to consider tax systems as a whole rather than assess its different elements in isolation. In practice, understanding the efficiency and equity effects of net wealth taxes requires taking interactions with the rest of the tax system into account. In countries with dual income tax systems that tax capital income at low and flat rates or in countries where capital gains are not taxed (e.g. Switzerland), there is a stronger justification for levying a net wealth tax. In those countries, the double taxation effect and the cumulative distortion (i.e. on top of capital income taxes) imposed by a net wealth tax are less evident. A similar argument can be made for countries that do not levy taxes on inheritances (e.g. Norway), although the effects of a low net wealth tax are likely to be much stronger than those of an inheritance tax, with even a low recurrent wealth tax liability resulting in high effective tax rates when the total amount of net wealth taxes paid is expressed as a share of taxpayers' estates.

In reviewing countries' practical experiences with net wealth taxes, the study reveals notable variations in tax design, but also identifies a number of common features and trends across countries. Variations in the levels of tax exemption thresholds have been significant, with some countries taxing exclusively the very wealthy and others taxing a broader range of taxpayers. Practices regarding tax rates have also varied. On the other hand, countries' experiences have revealed a number of common characteristics. Across countries, net wealth tax bases have generally been narrow because of numerous exemptions and reliefs, motivated by a variety of economic, social and practical concerns. Tax avoidance and evasion behaviours have also been widespread in all countries. Generally, countries' experiences confirm the difficulties involved in taxing net wealth on a recurrent basis. In the countries that still have net wealth taxes, there has also been a trend towards raising tax exemption thresholds and lowering tax rates. The former has been driven primarily by a desire to avoid burdening the middle/upper middle class, while the latter party reflects tax competition between countries or local governments in countries where net wealth taxes are local.

Net wealth taxes can be designed in ways that make them both less distortive and fairer. Regarding tax exemption thresholds and rates, recommendations depend on whether the net wealth tax comes on top of other taxes on capital, in particular on top of taxes on capital income. In the case of a wealth tax that comes on top of broad-based capital income taxes, tax exemption thresholds should be high, to ensure that the tax is only levied on the very wealthy, and tax rates should be low and take into account tax rates on capital income to avoid imposing excessively high tax burdens on capital. In cases where net wealth taxes do not come on top of broad-based capital income taxes, lower exemption thresholds and higher tax rates may be justified. Tax rates could be progressive, especially in cases where net wealth taxes do not come on top of capital income taxes and/or wealth transfer taxes, to enhance the overall tax system's progressivity.

Other recommendations that apply to all net wealth taxes include:

- Limited tax exemptions and reliefs;
- An exemption for business assets, with clear criteria restricting the availability of the exemption (ensuring that real business activity is taking place and that assets are directly being used in the taxpayer's professional activity)
- An exemption for personal and household effects up to a certain value;
- Determining the tax base based on asset market values; although the tax base could amount to a fixed percentage of that market value (e.g. 80-85%) to prevent valuation disputes and take into account costs that may be incurred to hold or maintain the assets
- Keeping the value of hard-to-value assets or the value of taxpayers' total net wealth constant for a few years to avoid yearly reassessments;
- Allowing debts to be deductible only if they have been incurred to acquire taxable assets – or, if the tax exemption threshold is high, consider further limiting debt deductibility;
- Measures allowing payments in instalments for taxpayers facing liquidity constraints;
- Ensuring transparency in the treatment of assets held in trusts;
- Continued efforts to enhance tax transparency and exchange information on the assets that residents hold in other jurisdictions;
- Developing third-party reporting;
- Establishing rules to prevent international double wealth taxation; and
- Regularly evaluating the effects of the wealth tax.

In addition, this report suggests that information about household wealth could be used in the design of other taxes. Income tax allowances or credits as well as benefit entitlements typically depend on income levels and the family status, but not on household wealth. This suggests scope for increased wealth-testing. For instance, mortgage interest relief and private pension tax incentives could be made income and wealth dependent. Information about total household wealth could also be used in the design of other property taxes and personal capital income taxes. Future work could explore ways in which wealth testing could be used to improve the design of taxes levied at the individual level.

This report also paves the way for future work on:

- The design of inheritance taxes
- The design of capital gains taxes
- The distributional effects of recurrent taxes on immovable property

- The use of wealth-testing for other tax and benefit purposes. In particular, the design and evaluation of recurrent immovable property tax rates and PIT rates which increase with both income and wealth levels
- The evaluation of accrual- versus realisation-based taxation within PIT systems – accrual-based PIT design to prevent lock-in effects
- Further work on the drivers of wealth inequality with a particular focus on the extent to which capital income taxes can contribute to a more equal wealth distribution

- [illegible] use of wealth [illegible] for other tax and benefit purposes, in particular the design and evaluation of [illegible] immovable property tax rates and PIT [illegible] which increase with both income and wealth levels.
- The evaluation of [illegible] PIT system [illegible] based PIT [illegible]
- [illegible]

Annex A. OECD questionnaire on current and historical net wealth taxes

Box A A.1. Questionnaire instructions

This questionnaire aims to collect information on the design of net wealth taxes as well as on their rationale and effects. Replies to the questionnaire will be used as input to the OECD Secretariat's report on Net Wealth Taxes in OECD Countries.

Please note that recurrent taxes on net wealth refer in this questionnaire to ***national and subnational recurrent taxes on individual net wealth****, i.e. taxes on a wide range of movable and immovable property, net of debt. Individual net wealth taxes are reported either under category 4200 (aggregated) or category 4210 (individual) in Revenue Statistics.*

All delegates are requested to reply to questions 1 and 2*. The rest of the questionnaire is only intended for countries that currently have or previously had net wealth taxes. Countries that currently have a net wealth tax are asked to provide information on their current net wealth tax. Countries that had a net wealth tax in the past are also requested to provide information on the design of their wealth tax prior to its repeal.*

Screening questions:

All delegates are requested to reply to questions 1 and 2.

1. Does your country currently have a recurrent tax on individual net wealth?

☐ Yes

☐ No

2. Did your country have a recurrent tax on individual net wealth between 1965 and 2016?

☐ Yes

☐ No

If you responded yes to either question 1 or 2, please proceed to the following questions.

PART 1 | GENERAL INFORMATION AND RATIONALE

General information

3. Name of the tax (in national language and English): ____

4. Year of introduction: ____

5. Year of abolition if the tax was repealed: ____

6. Was the net wealth tax initially introduced as a temporary measure?

☐ Yes

☐ No

7. National tax or local/municipal tax:

☐ National level tax

☐ Local/municipal level tax

☐ National and local/municipal tax

Rationale

8. Main rationale for introducing the net wealth tax: ____

9. If the net wealth tax is still in force, main rationale for maintaining it: ____

10. If the net wealth tax was repealed, main rationale for repealing it: ____

PART 2 | NET WEALTH TAX DESIGN

Tax base

11. The tax applies on:

☐ An individual basis

☐ A family basis

12. Tax base for residents, please specify if other than worldwide net assets: ___

13. Tax base for non-residents, please specify if other than assets that are physically located within the jurisdiction: ___

14. Taxed assets, please list (e.g. residential property; land; movable property; listed and unlisted shares; corporate and government bonds; cash, etc.):

- __
- __
- etc.

15. Untaxed assets, please specify (e.g. business assets; pension savings; assets held in collective investment vehicles, trusts and foundations; jewellery; artwork; vehicles; intellectual property rights; etc.): ___

16. For business assets, please specify those which are exempt:

☐ Assets directly used in the professional activity of the taxpayer, please specify rules: ___

☐ Shares in a company owned by the taxpayer (and possibly relatives), please specify rules: ___

☐ Other, please specify: ___

17. Valuation rules, please specify valuation rules for all taxable assets:

- __

- __
- etc.

18. Is there an exemption threshold?

☐ No

☐ Yes, based on the value of total net taxable assets, please specify (in national currency): __

☐ Yes, based on taxpayer income, please specify (in national currency): __

19. Tax allowances, please specify:

- __
- __
- etc.

20. Tax credits, please specify:

- __
- __
- etc.

21. Deductibility of debts, please specify deductible and non-deductible debts:

- Deductible debts: ___
- Non-deductible debts: ___

22. Tax cap or other limitations on total tax liability, if yes please specify rules: ___

23. Temporary exemption (net wealth tax holiday) for individuals/households who change their tax residency:

☐ Yes, please specify rules: ____

☐ No

24. Were the above rules previously different? If so, please specify thc main net wealth tax base changes that were introduced and why ___

Tax rates

25. Please specify applicable tax rates (for local or municipal level taxes, please provide as much information as possible):

Value of table assets (in nat. currency)	Tax rates (%)

26. Were the above tax rates previously different? If so, please specify the main net wealth tax rate changes that were introduced and why___

Tax filing and administration

27. Self-assessment:

☐ Yes

☐ No

28. Tax return:

☐ Separate wealth tax return

☐ Tax return consolidated with income tax return

29. Please specify penalties for late filing, late payment, incorrect statements and non-declarations: ___

30. What are the main challenges faced by the government in administering the net wealth tax? ___

31. Given that the tax administration collects taxpayer information on wealth, is that information used in other tax areas (e.g. asset-testing for income tax purposes)?

☐ Yes, please specify ___

☐ No

PART 3 | EFFECTS OF THE NET WEALTH TAX

Tax revenues

32. Revenues from the net wealth tax in 2016 (or last available year if the tax was repealed or if 2016 data is not yet available) in national currency [*For reference, please see the tax revenues reported by your country in 2015 in Annex A*]: ___

33. Estimated revenue loss from net wealth tax expenditures (if available) in national currency: ___

Number of taxpayers

34. Number of individuals/households liable to the net wealth tax in 2016 (or last available year if the tax was repealed): ___

Tax avoidance/evasion and fiscal expatriation

35. Please describe the most common used avoidance and evasion schemes in your country (e.g. avoidance through trusts, holding assets in corporations, avoidance through gifts, avoidance through charitable donations, etc.): ___

36. What are the main rules in place to prevent those schemes and other forms of avoidance/evasion? ___

37. Has the government undertaken an evaluation of the avoidance and evasion effects of the net wealth tax?

☐ Yes

☐ No

38. Has the government undertaken an evaluation of the effects of the net wealth tax on the tax residence decisions of taxpayers (i.e. fiscal expatriation)?

☐ Yes

☐ No

39. Estimations of net wealth tax fraud and fiscal expatriation:

	Estimation	Year(s)
Revenue loss from wealth tax fraud	____ (in nat. currency)	
Revenue loss from fiscal expatriation	____ (in nat. currency)	
Number of "fiscal expatriates"	____ (in nat. currency)	

40. Please provide us with any available internal assessments and external studies on wealth tax avoidance/evasion and fiscal expatriation in your country.

Growth/efficiency and redistribution

41. Has the government undertaken an evaluation of the effects of the net wealth tax on growth?

☐ Yes

☐ No

42. Has the government undertaken an evaluation of the effects of the net wealth tax on the total amount and composition of savings?

☐ Yes

☐ No

43. Has the government undertaken an evaluation of the redistributive effects of the net wealth tax?

☐ Yes

☐ No

44. Please provide us with any available internal assessments and external studies on the efficiency/growth and redistributive effects of the wealth tax.

ORGANISATION FOR ECONOMIC CO-OPERATION AND DEVELOPMENT

The OECD is a unique forum where governments work together to address the economic, social and environmental challenges of globalisation. The OECD is also at the forefront of efforts to understand and to help governments respond to new developments and concerns, such as corporate governance, the information economy and the challenges of an ageing population. The Organisation provides a setting where governments can compare policy experiences, seek answers to common problems, identify good practice and work to co-ordinate domestic and international policies.

The OECD member countries are: Australia, Austria, Belgium, Canada, Chile, the Czech Republic, Denmark, Estonia, Finland, France, Germany, Greece, Hungary, Iceland, Ireland, Israel, Italy, Japan, Korea, Latvia, Luxembourg, Mexico, the Netherlands, New Zealand, Norway, Poland, Portugal, the Slovak Republic, Slovenia, Spain, Sweden, Switzerland, Turkey, the United Kingdom and the United States. The European Union takes part in the work of the OECD.

OECD Publishing disseminates widely the results of the Organisation's statistics gathering and research on economic, social and environmental issues, as well as the conventions, guidelines and standards agreed by its members.

OECD PUBLISHING, 2, rue André-Pascal, 75775 PARIS CEDEX 16
(23 2018 06 1 P) ISBN 978-92-64-29029-7 – 2018

www.ingramcontent.com/pod-product-compliance
Lightning Source LLC
LaVergne TN
LVHW081413110826
845149LV00010B/1725

* 9 7 8 9 2 6 4 2 9 0 2 9 7 *